50 Movie Night Recipes for Home

By: Kelly Johnson

Table of Contents

- French Toast (France)
- Croissant (France)
- Eggs Benedict (United States)
- Pancakes with Maple Syrup (United States)
- Bagel with Cream Cheese and Lox (United States)
- Huevos Rancheros (Mexico)
- Chilaquiles (Mexico)
- Empanadas (Argentina)
- Açaí Bowl (Brazil)
- Pastel de Nata (Portugal)
- Full English Breakfast (United Kingdom)
- Scottish Porridge (Scotland)
- Irish Breakfast (Ireland)
- Swedish Pancakes (Sweden)
- Danish Pastries (Denmark)
- Greek Yogurt with Honey and Nuts (Greece)
- Shakshuka (Middle East)
- Turkish Breakfast Platter (Turkey)
- Congee (China)
- Dim Sum (China)
- Bánh Mì (Vietnam)
- Pho (Vietnam)
- Kimchi Fried Rice (Korea)
- Onigiri (Japan)
- Miso Soup (Japan)
- Aussie Breakfast Pie (Australia)
- Vegemite on Toast (Australia)
- Lamingtons (Australia)
- Kiwi Fruit Salad (New Zealand)
- Canadian Bacon and Eggs (Canada)
- BeaverTails (Canada)
- Poutine (Canada)
- Smørrebrød (Denmark)
- Kedgeree (India)
- Masala Dosa (India)

- Idli with Sambar (India)
- Roti Canai (Malaysia)
- Nasi Lemak (Malaysia)
- Laksa (Singapore)
- Hainanese Chicken Rice (Singapore)
- Kaya Toast (Singapore)
- Arroz con Leche (Spain)
- Tortilla Española (Spain)
- Pan con Tomate (Spain)
- Welsh Rarebit (Wales)
- Biscuits and Gravy (United States)
- Tex-Mex Migas (United States)
- Cuban Sandwich (Cuba)
- Colombian Arepas (Colombia)
- Venezuelan Arepas (Venezuela)

French Toast (France)

Ingredients:

- 4 thick slices of bread (preferably stale)
- 2 large eggs
- 1/2 cup milk
- 1 teaspoon vanilla extract
- 1/2 teaspoon ground cinnamon
- Butter or oil for frying
- Maple syrup, powdered sugar, or fresh fruits for serving (optional)

Instructions:

1. In a shallow dish, whisk together eggs, milk, vanilla extract, and ground cinnamon until well combined.
2. Dip each slice of bread into the egg mixture, allowing it to soak for about 20-30 seconds on each side. Ensure the bread is evenly coated with the mixture.
3. Heat a skillet or frying pan over medium heat and add a little butter or oil.
4. Place the soaked bread slices in the skillet and cook until golden brown on both sides, about 2-3 minutes per side.
5. Once cooked, transfer the French toast to a plate and serve immediately with your choice of toppings such as maple syrup, powdered sugar, or fresh fruits.

Enjoy your delicious French Toast, reminiscent of breakfasts in France!

Croissant (France)

Ingredients:

- 2 1/4 teaspoons (1 packet) active dry yeast
- 1/4 cup warm water (110°F/45°C)
- 1/2 cup cold milk
- 1/3 cup granulated sugar
- 1 teaspoon salt

- 2 1/2 cups all-purpose flour, plus more for dusting
- 1 cup (2 sticks) unsalted butter, cold
- 1 egg, beaten (for egg wash)

Instructions:

1. In a small bowl, dissolve the yeast in the warm water and let it sit for about 5 minutes until foamy.
2. In a large mixing bowl, combine the yeast mixture, cold milk, sugar, salt, and flour. Stir until a dough forms.
3. Turn the dough out onto a floured surface and knead for about 5 minutes until smooth and elastic. Shape the dough into a ball and place it in a lightly greased bowl. Cover with plastic wrap and let it rise in a warm place for about 1 hour, or until doubled in size.
4. While the dough is rising, prepare the butter layer. Place the cold butter between two sheets of parchment paper and pound it with a rolling pin until it forms a 6x6-inch square. Chill the butter square in the refrigerator until firm but still pliable.
5. Once the dough has doubled in size, punch it down and roll it out on a floured surface into a 12x12-inch square. Place the chilled butter square diagonally onto the dough square and fold the corners of the dough over the butter, sealing it inside.
6. Roll out the dough into a 20x10-inch rectangle. Fold the dough into thirds like a letter, then turn it 90 degrees and roll it out again into a 20x10-inch rectangle. Fold it into thirds again.
7. Wrap the dough in plastic wrap and refrigerate for at least 1 hour, or overnight.
8. After chilling, roll out the dough into a 16x8-inch rectangle. Cut the rectangle into triangles.
9. Roll each triangle up tightly, starting from the wide end, to form croissants. Place them on a baking sheet lined with parchment paper, with the pointed end tucked underneath.
10. Cover the croissants loosely with plastic wrap and let them rise in a warm place for about 1-2 hours, until puffed and almost doubled in size.
11. Preheat the oven to 400°F (200°C). Brush the risen croissants with the beaten egg wash.
12. Bake the croissants for 15-20 minutes, or until golden brown and flaky.
13. Allow the croissants to cool slightly before serving. Enjoy your homemade French croissants!

Note: This recipe requires some patience and precision, but the end result is delicious, buttery croissants that are perfect for breakfast or brunch.

Eggs Benedict (United States)

Ingredients:

For the Hollandaise Sauce:

- 3 large egg yolks
- 1 tablespoon water
- 1 tablespoon lemon juice
- 1/2 cup (1 stick) unsalted butter, melted
- Salt and pepper to taste
- Dash of cayenne pepper (optional)

For the Eggs Benedict:

- 4 English muffins, split and toasted
- 8 slices Canadian bacon or ham
- 8 large eggs
- Vinegar (for poaching eggs)
- Chopped fresh parsley (optional, for garnish)
- Paprika (optional, for garnish)

Instructions:

1. Prepare the Hollandaise Sauce: In a heatproof bowl, whisk together the egg yolks, water, and lemon juice until well combined.
2. Place the bowl over a pot of simmering water (double boiler method), ensuring that the bottom of the bowl does not touch the water.
3. Gradually whisk in the melted butter, pouring it in a slow, steady stream, until the sauce thickens and becomes smooth. Be sure to whisk constantly to prevent the eggs from scrambling.

4. Once the hollandaise sauce has thickened, season it with salt, pepper, and cayenne pepper (if using). Keep the sauce warm while you prepare the other components of the dish, but be careful not to let it get too hot or it may separate.
5. Prepare the Poached Eggs: Fill a large saucepan with water and bring it to a gentle simmer. Add a splash of vinegar to the water (about 1 tablespoon) to help the eggs hold their shape.
6. Crack each egg into a small bowl or ramekin. Using a spoon, create a gentle whirlpool in the simmering water, then carefully slide the eggs, one at a time, into the center of the whirlpool. Poach the eggs for about 3-4 minutes, or until the whites are set but the yolks are still runny.
7. Using a slotted spoon, remove the poached eggs from the water and transfer them to a plate lined with paper towels to drain any excess water.
8. Assemble the Eggs Benedict: Place the toasted English muffin halves on serving plates. Top each half with a slice of Canadian bacon or ham, followed by a poached egg.
9. Spoon the hollandaise sauce generously over the poached eggs.
10. Garnish with chopped fresh parsley and a sprinkle of paprika, if desired.
11. Serve immediately, and enjoy your homemade Eggs Benedict!

Note: Eggs Benedict is often served with a side of hash browns, roasted potatoes, or sautéed spinach. Feel free to customize the dish according to your preferences.

Pancakes with Maple Syrup (United States)

Ingredients:

- 1 1/2 cups all-purpose flour
- 3 1/2 teaspoons baking powder
- 1 teaspoon salt
- 1 tablespoon granulated sugar
- 1 1/4 cups milk
- 1 egg
- 3 tablespoons melted butter or vegetable oil
- Butter and maple syrup for serving

Instructions:

1. In a large mixing bowl, sift together the flour, baking powder, salt, and sugar.
2. In a separate bowl, whisk together the milk, egg, and melted butter or oil until well combined.
3. Pour the wet ingredients into the dry ingredients and stir until just combined. Be careful not to overmix; a few lumps in the batter are okay.
4. Heat a non-stick skillet or griddle over medium heat. Lightly grease the skillet with butter or oil.
5. Pour about 1/4 cup of batter onto the skillet for each pancake. Cook until bubbles form on the surface of the pancake and the edges begin to look set, about 2-3 minutes.
6. Flip the pancakes and cook for an additional 1-2 minutes on the other side, or until golden brown and cooked through.
7. Repeat with the remaining batter, greasing the skillet as needed.
8. Serve the pancakes warm with butter and maple syrup drizzled on top.
9. Enjoy your homemade pancakes with maple syrup, a classic American breakfast treat!

Note: You can customize these pancakes by adding toppings such as fresh berries, sliced bananas, chocolate chips, or chopped nuts before flipping them. Feel free to get creative and make them your own!

Bagel with Cream Cheese and Lox (United States)

Ingredients:

- 4 bagels (plain, sesame, or everything)
- 8 ounces cream cheese, softened
- 8 ounces smoked salmon (lox), thinly sliced
- 1 small red onion, thinly sliced
- Capers, for garnish (optional)
- Fresh dill, for garnish (optional)
- Lemon wedges, for serving (optional)

Instructions:

1. Slice the bagels in half horizontally and toast them to your desired level of crispiness.
2. Spread a generous amount of cream cheese on each half of the toasted bagels.
3. Top each half with slices of smoked salmon (lox).
4. Arrange a few slices of red onion on top of the salmon.
5. If desired, sprinkle capers over the onions for an extra burst of flavor.
6. Garnish with fresh dill for added freshness.
7. Serve the bagels with lemon wedges on the side for squeezing over the salmon, if desired.
8. Enjoy your homemade bagels with cream cheese and lox, a delicious and satisfying breakfast or brunch option!

Feel free to customize your bagels with additional toppings such as sliced tomatoes, cucumber, or avocado, according to your preferences.

Huevos Rancheros (Mexico)

Ingredients:

- 4 corn tortillas
- 4 large eggs
- 1 cup refried beans (homemade or canned)
- 1 cup salsa (homemade or store-bought)
- 1/2 cup shredded cheese (such as cheddar or Monterey Jack)
- 1 avocado, sliced
- Fresh cilantro, chopped, for garnish
- Lime wedges, for serving
- Salt and pepper, to taste
- Olive oil or cooking spray

Instructions:

1. Warm the tortillas: Heat a large skillet over medium heat and warm the tortillas for about 1 minute on each side until they are soft and pliable. Keep them warm by wrapping them in a clean kitchen towel or aluminum foil.

2. Cook the eggs: In the same skillet, add a little olive oil or cooking spray. Crack the eggs into the skillet and cook them to your desired doneness (fried or sunny-side-up). Season with salt and pepper.
3. Heat the refried beans: In a small saucepan, heat the refried beans over medium-low heat until warmed through. Stir occasionally to prevent sticking.
4. Assemble the Huevos Rancheros: Place a warm tortilla on each plate. Spread a layer of warm refried beans on top of each tortilla. Top the beans with a fried egg.
5. Spoon salsa over each egg, and sprinkle shredded cheese on top.
6. Garnish with sliced avocado and chopped cilantro.
7. Serve immediately with lime wedges on the side for squeezing over the Huevos Rancheros.
8. Enjoy your homemade Huevos Rancheros, a flavorful and satisfying Mexican breakfast dish!

Feel free to customize your Huevos Rancheros with additional toppings such as sliced jalapeños, diced tomatoes, or a dollop of sour cream, according to your taste preferences.

Chilaquiles (Mexico)

Ingredients:

- 8 corn tortillas, cut into wedges or strips
- 2 cups salsa (homemade or store-bought)
- 2 tablespoons vegetable oil
- 1 cup cooked shredded chicken (optional)
- 1/2 cup crumbled queso fresco or shredded cheese (such as Monterey Jack or cheddar)
- 4 large eggs
- 1 avocado, sliced
- 1/4 cup chopped fresh cilantro, for garnish
- Lime wedges, for serving
- Salt and pepper, to taste

Instructions:

1. Preheat your oven to 350°F (175°C).
2. In a large skillet, heat the vegetable oil over medium-high heat. Once hot, add the tortilla wedges or strips in batches, frying until they are golden and crispy. Remove the fried tortillas from the skillet and place them on a paper towel-lined plate to drain any excess oil.
3. In the same skillet, add the salsa and bring it to a simmer. If using shredded chicken, add it to the salsa and stir to combine.
4. Add the fried tortilla chips to the skillet with the salsa, tossing gently to coat the chips evenly. Allow the chips to simmer in the salsa for a few minutes until they soften slightly but are not mushy.
5. While the tortilla chips are simmering, prepare the eggs. You can either fry, scramble, or poach the eggs according to your preference.
6. Once the tortilla chips are coated with the salsa and have softened slightly, sprinkle the crumbled queso fresco or shredded cheese over the top.
7. Create wells in the mixture and carefully crack the eggs into the skillet, spacing them evenly apart. Cover the skillet with a lid or foil and cook for a few minutes until the eggs are cooked to your desired doneness and the cheese is melted.
8. Remove the skillet from the heat and garnish the Chilaquiles with sliced avocado and chopped fresh cilantro.
9. Serve the Chilaquiles hot, directly from the skillet, with lime wedges on the side for squeezing over the dish.
10. Enjoy your homemade Chilaquiles, a flavorful and comforting Mexican breakfast dish!

Feel free to customize your Chilaquiles with additional toppings such as sliced jalapeños, diced tomatoes, sour cream, or sliced radishes, according to your taste preferences.

Empanadas (Argentina)

Ingredients:

For the dough:

- 3 cups all-purpose flour

- 1 teaspoon salt
- 1/2 cup unsalted butter, cold and cut into small cubes
- 1/2 cup water, cold
- 1 egg, beaten (for egg wash)

For the filling:

- 1 tablespoon olive oil
- 1 onion, finely chopped
- 2 cloves garlic, minced
- 1 pound ground beef
- 1 teaspoon paprika
- 1 teaspoon ground cumin
- 1/2 teaspoon dried oregano
- Salt and pepper, to taste
- 1/2 cup green olives, pitted and chopped
- 2 hard-boiled eggs, chopped
- Optional: 1/2 cup raisins or chopped bell peppers

Instructions:

1. Prepare the dough: In a large mixing bowl, combine the flour and salt. Add the cold butter cubes and use your fingers or a pastry cutter to rub the butter into the flour until the mixture resembles coarse crumbs.
2. Gradually add the cold water, mixing until a dough forms. Knead the dough gently on a floured surface for a few minutes until smooth. Wrap the dough in plastic wrap and refrigerate for at least 30 minutes.
3. Prepare the filling: In a skillet, heat the olive oil over medium heat. Add the chopped onion and garlic, and cook until softened, about 5 minutes.
4. Add the ground beef to the skillet and cook until browned, breaking it up with a spoon as it cooks.
5. Stir in the paprika, cumin, oregano, salt, and pepper, and cook for another 2-3 minutes to toast the spices.
6. Remove the skillet from the heat and stir in the chopped olives and hard-boiled eggs. If using, add the raisins or chopped bell peppers. Allow the filling to cool slightly.

7. Preheat your oven to 375°F (190°C) and line a baking sheet with parchment paper.
8. Roll out the chilled dough on a floured surface to about 1/8 inch thickness. Use a round cutter (about 4-6 inches in diameter) to cut out circles of dough.
9. Place a spoonful of the beef filling in the center of each dough circle. Fold the dough over the filling to create a half-moon shape, and press the edges together to seal. You can crimp the edges with a fork for a decorative touch.
10. Transfer the filled empanadas to the prepared baking sheet. Brush the tops with beaten egg wash.
11. Bake the empanadas in the preheated oven for 20-25 minutes, or until golden brown and crispy.
12. Remove from the oven and let cool slightly before serving.
13. Enjoy your homemade Argentine beef empanadas, either as a snack, appetizer, or main course!

Feel free to customize the filling with your favorite ingredients, and experiment with different shapes and sizes for your empanadas.

Açaí Bowl (Brazil)

Ingredients:

For the açaí base:

- 2 packs (about 200g each) frozen unsweetened açaí pulp or açaí puree
- 1 ripe banana, sliced and frozen
- 1/2 cup frozen mixed berries (such as strawberries, blueberries, or raspberries)
- 1/2 cup unsweetened almond milk or coconut water
- 1 tablespoon honey or maple syrup (optional, for added sweetness)

For the toppings:

- Granola
- Sliced fresh fruit (such as bananas, strawberries, kiwi, or mango)
- Nut butter (such as almond or peanut butter)
- Chopped nuts (such as almonds, walnuts, or cashews)

- Seeds (such as chia seeds, hemp seeds, or pumpkin seeds)
- Shredded coconut
- Honey or maple syrup, for drizzling (optional)

Instructions:

1. In a blender, combine the frozen açaí pulp, frozen banana slices, frozen mixed berries, almond milk or coconut water, and honey or maple syrup (if using). Blend until smooth and creamy, scraping down the sides of the blender as needed. The consistency should be thick like a soft-serve ice cream.
2. Pour the blended açaí mixture into serving bowls.
3. Arrange the toppings on top of the açaí base. Start with a generous sprinkle of granola, followed by sliced fresh fruit, nut butter, chopped nuts, seeds, and shredded coconut. Drizzle with honey or maple syrup for added sweetness, if desired.
4. Serve immediately and enjoy your homemade açaí bowl!

Note: Açaí bowls are highly customizable, so feel free to get creative with your toppings and adjust the ingredients according to your preferences. You can also add extras like yogurt, cocoa nibs, or dried fruit for added flavor and texture.

Pastel de Nata (Portugal)

Ingredients:

For the pastry:

- 1 sheet puff pastry (store-bought or homemade)

For the custard filling:

- 1 cup whole milk
- 1/2 cup heavy cream
- 1/3 cup granulated sugar
- 2 tablespoons all-purpose flour

- 4 large egg yolks
- 1 teaspoon vanilla extract
- Zest of 1 lemon (optional)

For dusting:

- Powdered sugar (optional)
- Ground cinnamon (optional)

Instructions:

1. Preheat your oven to 475°F (245°C). Grease a standard muffin tin or line it with parchment paper liners.
2. Roll out the puff pastry on a lightly floured surface until it's about 1/8 inch thick. Using a round cutter or a glass, cut out circles of pastry dough that are slightly larger than the muffin tin cups. Press each circle of dough into the muffin tin cups, shaping them to fit snugly. Prick the bottoms of the pastry shells with a fork to prevent them from puffing up too much during baking.
3. In a saucepan, heat the milk and heavy cream over medium heat until it begins to simmer. Do not let it boil.
4. In a separate bowl, whisk together the sugar, flour, egg yolks, vanilla extract, and lemon zest (if using) until smooth and well combined.
5. Slowly pour the hot milk mixture into the egg mixture, whisking constantly to prevent the eggs from curdling. Continue whisking until the mixture is smooth.
6. Pour the custard mixture through a fine-mesh sieve into a clean saucepan to remove any lumps.
7. Cook the custard mixture over medium heat, stirring constantly, until it thickens to a pudding-like consistency, about 5-7 minutes. Remove from heat and let the custard cool slightly.
8. Spoon the custard filling into the prepared pastry shells, filling each one almost to the top.
9. Bake the Pastel de Nata in the preheated oven for 12-15 minutes, or until the pastry is golden brown and the custard is set with a slight jiggle in the center.
10. Remove the Pastel de Nata from the oven and let them cool in the muffin tin for a few minutes before transferring them to a wire rack to cool completely.
11. Once cooled, dust the Pastel de Nata with powdered sugar and ground cinnamon, if desired.

12. Serve the Pastel de Nata at room temperature or slightly warm, and enjoy these delicious Portuguese custard tarts as a sweet treat or dessert!

Note: Pastel de Nata is best enjoyed on the day it's made, but leftovers can be stored in an airtight container in the refrigerator for up to 2 days. Warm them up in the oven before serving, if desired.

Full English Breakfast (United Kingdom)

Ingredients:

- 4 large eggs
- 4 slices of bacon
- 4 pork sausages
- 1 can (about 400g) baked beans
- 2 large tomatoes, halved
- 8 button mushrooms, halved
- 4 slices of bread (white or wholemeal), toasted
- Butter, for spreading
- Salt and pepper, to taste
- Optional: black pudding, hash browns, fried bread

Instructions:

1. Preheat your oven to 400°F (200°C). Arrange the bacon slices, sausages, halved tomatoes, and halved mushrooms on a baking sheet lined with parchment paper. Season the tomatoes and mushrooms with salt and pepper.
2. Roast the bacon, sausages, tomatoes, and mushrooms in the preheated oven for 20-25 minutes, or until the bacon is crispy, the sausages are cooked through, and the vegetables are tender.
3. While the ingredients are roasting, heat the baked beans in a saucepan over medium heat until heated through.
4. Heat a non-stick skillet over medium heat and fry the eggs to your desired doneness (fried, scrambled, or poached). Season with salt and pepper.
5. Toast the slices of bread until golden brown, then spread butter on each slice.

6. Once all the components are cooked, assemble the Full English Breakfast on serving plates. Divide the bacon, sausages, tomatoes, mushrooms, and toast between the plates. Spoon the heated baked beans onto each plate.
7. Serve the Full English Breakfast immediately, and enjoy this hearty and satisfying meal!

Optional additions to consider:

- Black pudding: A traditional British sausage made from pork blood and oatmeal, often fried or grilled.
- Hash browns: Grated and fried potatoes formed into patties.
- Fried bread: Slices of bread fried in butter or oil until golden and crispy.

Feel free to customize your Full English Breakfast with additional ingredients or variations according to your preferences. It's a versatile meal that can be adapted to suit individual tastes.

Scottish Porridge (Scotland)

Ingredients:

- 1 cup steel-cut oats (traditional Scottish oats)
- 3 cups water or milk (or a combination of both)
- Pinch of salt (optional)
- Optional toppings: honey, maple syrup, brown sugar, fresh berries, sliced bananas, chopped nuts, cinnamon, etc.

Instructions:

1. In a medium saucepan, bring the water or milk (or a combination of both) to a boil over medium-high heat.
2. Once the liquid is boiling, add a pinch of salt (if using) and stir in the steel-cut oats.

3. Reduce the heat to low and simmer the oats, stirring occasionally, for about 20-30 minutes, or until the oats are thick and creamy. Be sure to stir frequently to prevent the oats from sticking to the bottom of the pan.
4. Once the porridge reaches your desired consistency, remove it from the heat.
5. Serve the Scottish porridge hot, either plain or topped with your favorite toppings. Common toppings include honey, maple syrup, brown sugar, fresh berries, sliced bananas, chopped nuts, or a sprinkle of cinnamon.
6. Enjoy your homemade Scottish porridge as a comforting and nutritious breakfast to start your day!

Note: You can adjust the consistency of the porridge by adding more or less liquid according to your preference. If you prefer a creamier texture, you can also stir in a splash of cream or milk at the end of cooking. Additionally, feel free to customize your porridge with additional flavorings such as vanilla extract, almond extract, or spices like nutmeg or ginger.

Irish Breakfast (Ireland)

Ingredients:

- 4 large eggs
- 4 slices of bacon (rashers)
- 4 pork sausages
- 2 slices of black pudding
- 2 slices of white pudding
- 1 can (about 400g) baked beans
- 2 large tomatoes, halved
- 8 button mushrooms, halved
- 4 slices of bread (white or brown), toasted
- Butter, for spreading
- Salt and pepper, to taste
- Optional: hash browns, fried potatoes, fried onions

Instructions:

1. Preheat your oven to 400°F (200°C). Arrange the bacon slices, sausages, black pudding, white pudding, halved tomatoes, and halved mushrooms on a baking sheet lined with parchment paper.
2. Roast the bacon, sausages, black pudding, white pudding, tomatoes, and mushrooms in the preheated oven for 20-25 minutes, or until the bacon is crispy, the sausages are cooked through, and the vegetables are tender.
3. While the ingredients are roasting, heat the baked beans in a saucepan over medium heat until heated through.
4. Heat a non-stick skillet over medium heat and fry the eggs to your desired doneness (fried, scrambled, or poached). Season with salt and pepper.
5. Toast the slices of bread until golden brown, then spread butter on each slice.
6. Once all the components are cooked, assemble the Irish breakfast on serving plates. Divide the bacon, sausages, black pudding, white pudding, tomatoes, mushrooms, and toast between the plates. Spoon the heated baked beans onto each plate.
7. Serve the Irish breakfast immediately, and enjoy this hearty and satisfying meal!

Optional additions to consider:

- Hash browns or fried potatoes: Grated and fried potatoes formed into patties or diced and fried until crispy.
- Fried onions: Sliced onions fried until golden and caramelized.

Feel free to customize your Irish breakfast with additional ingredients or variations according to your preferences. It's a versatile meal that can be adapted to suit individual tastes.

Swedish Pancakes (Sweden)

Ingredients:

- 1 cup all-purpose flour
- 2 tablespoons granulated sugar
- 1/4 teaspoon salt
- 2 large eggs

- 1 1/2 cups milk
- 2 tablespoons unsalted butter, melted
- Butter or oil, for greasing the skillet
- Lingonberry jam, whipped cream, fresh berries, or powdered sugar, for serving (optional)

Instructions:

1. In a large mixing bowl, whisk together the flour, sugar, and salt.
2. In a separate bowl, beat the eggs, then whisk in the milk and melted butter until well combined.
3. Gradually pour the wet ingredients into the dry ingredients, whisking constantly, until a smooth batter forms. Let the batter rest for about 10-15 minutes to allow the flour to hydrate.
4. Heat a non-stick skillet or crepe pan over medium heat. Lightly grease the skillet with butter or oil.
5. Pour a small ladleful of batter into the skillet, swirling it around to evenly coat the bottom in a thin layer.
6. Cook the pancake for 1-2 minutes, or until the edges begin to lift and the bottom is lightly golden brown.
7. Using a spatula, carefully flip the pancake and cook for an additional 1-2 minutes on the other side, until golden brown and cooked through.
8. Transfer the cooked pancake to a plate and keep warm. Repeat the process with the remaining batter, greasing the skillet as needed.
9. Serve the Swedish pancakes warm, folded or rolled, with your choice of toppings such as lingonberry jam, whipped cream, fresh berries, or powdered sugar.
10. Enjoy your homemade Swedish pancakes, a delicious and versatile dish that can be enjoyed for breakfast, brunch, or dessert!

Note: Swedish pancakes can be made ahead of time and reheated in a low oven or microwave before serving. They can also be stored in the refrigerator for a few days or frozen for longer storage.

Danish Pastries (Denmark)

Ingredients:

For the dough:

- 2 1/4 teaspoons (1 packet) active dry yeast
- 1/4 cup warm water (about 110°F/45°C)
- 1/2 cup milk, at room temperature
- 1/4 cup granulated sugar
- 1 teaspoon salt
- 1 large egg, beaten
- 2 1/2 cups all-purpose flour
- 1 cup (2 sticks) unsalted butter, cold

For the filling (choose one):

- Fruit jam or preserves
- Almond paste
- Pastry cream or custard

For the glaze:

- 1 cup powdered sugar
- 2-3 tablespoons milk or water
- 1/2 teaspoon vanilla extract (optional)

Instructions:

1. In a small bowl, dissolve the yeast in the warm water and let it sit for about 5 minutes until foamy.
2. In a large mixing bowl or the bowl of a stand mixer fitted with a dough hook, combine the yeast mixture, milk, sugar, salt, and beaten egg. Gradually add the flour, mixing until a dough forms.

3. Turn the dough out onto a lightly floured surface and knead it for about 5 minutes until smooth and elastic. Alternatively, knead the dough in the stand mixer for about 3-4 minutes.
4. Shape the dough into a ball and place it in a lightly greased bowl. Cover with plastic wrap and let it rise in a warm place for about 1 hour, or until doubled in size.
5. While the dough is rising, prepare the butter block. Place the cold butter between two sheets of parchment paper and pound it with a rolling pin until it forms a 6x6-inch square. Chill the butter square in the refrigerator until firm but still pliable.
6. Once the dough has doubled in size, punch it down and roll it out on a floured surface into a 12x12-inch square.
7. Place the chilled butter square diagonally onto the dough square and fold the corners of the dough over the butter, sealing it inside.
8. Roll out the dough into a 20x10-inch rectangle. Fold the dough into thirds like a letter, then turn it 90 degrees and roll it out again into a 20x10-inch rectangle. Fold it into thirds again.
9. Wrap the dough in plastic wrap and refrigerate for at least 1 hour, or overnight.
10. After chilling, roll out the dough into a 16x8-inch rectangle. Cut the rectangle into squares or rectangles, depending on the size of Danish pastries you prefer.
11. Place a spoonful of your chosen filling in the center of each dough square. Fold the corners of the dough over the filling to form a pocket or envelope shape.
12. Transfer the filled pastries to a baking sheet lined with parchment paper, leaving space between each pastry.
13. Preheat your oven to 400°F (200°C). Let the filled pastries rise for about 20-30 minutes while the oven is preheating.
14. Bake the Danish pastries in the preheated oven for 15-20 minutes, or until golden brown and puffed up.
15. While the pastries are baking, prepare the glaze by whisking together the powdered sugar, milk or water, and vanilla extract (if using) until smooth.
16. Once the pastries are done baking, remove them from the oven and let them cool slightly on a wire rack. Drizzle the glaze over the warm pastries.
17. Serve the Danish pastries warm or at room temperature, and enjoy your homemade Wienerbrød!

Note: Danish pastries can be filled with various sweet fillings such as fruit jam, almond paste, or pastry cream. Feel free to experiment with different fillings and shapes to create your own unique Danish pastries.

Greek Yogurt with Honey and Nuts (Greece)

Ingredients:

- 1 cup Greek yogurt
- 1-2 tablespoons honey (adjust to taste)
- 2 tablespoons chopped nuts (such as walnuts, almonds, or pistachios)
- Optional: fresh fruit (such as berries or sliced bananas) for garnish

Instructions:

1. Spoon the Greek yogurt into a serving bowl.
2. Drizzle the honey over the yogurt, adjusting the amount to your desired level of sweetness.
3. Sprinkle the chopped nuts over the yogurt and honey.
4. If desired, garnish with fresh fruit such as berries or sliced bananas for added flavor and texture.
5. Serve the Greek yogurt with honey and nuts immediately, and enjoy this simple and nutritious breakfast or snack!

Note: Feel free to customize your Greek yogurt with honey and nuts by using different types of nuts or adding additional toppings such as granola, seeds, or dried fruit. You can also experiment with flavored Greek yogurt or different varieties of honey for a unique twist.

Shakshuka (Middle East)

Ingredients:

- 2 tablespoons olive oil
- 1 onion, finely chopped
- 2 bell peppers (red, yellow, or orange), diced
- 3 cloves garlic, minced
- 1 teaspoon ground cumin
- 1 teaspoon smoked paprika
- 1/2 teaspoon cayenne pepper (optional, for heat)
- 1 can (14 ounces) diced tomatoes
- 1 can (6 ounces) tomato paste
- Salt and pepper, to taste
- 4-6 large eggs
- Fresh parsley or cilantro, chopped, for garnish
- Crumbled feta cheese, for garnish (optional)
- Crusty bread or pita, for serving

Instructions:

1. Heat the olive oil in a large skillet or cast-iron pan over medium heat. Add the chopped onion and diced bell peppers. Cook, stirring occasionally, until the vegetables are softened, about 5-7 minutes.
2. Add the minced garlic, ground cumin, smoked paprika, and cayenne pepper (if using) to the skillet. Cook, stirring constantly, for 1-2 minutes until fragrant.
3. Stir in the diced tomatoes and tomato paste. Season the mixture with salt and pepper to taste. Allow the sauce to simmer gently for about 10-15 minutes, until it thickens slightly.
4. Using a spoon, make small indentations in the sauce for the eggs. Crack each egg into a small bowl or cup, then carefully pour each egg into one of the indentations in the sauce.
5. Cover the skillet with a lid and let the eggs cook in the sauce for about 5-7 minutes, or until the egg whites are set but the yolks are still runny. If you prefer firmer yolks, cook the eggs for longer.
6. Once the eggs are cooked to your liking, remove the skillet from the heat. Sprinkle chopped parsley or cilantro over the top, and crumble feta cheese (if using) for added flavor.
7. Serve the Shakshuka hot, directly from the skillet, with crusty bread or pita on the side for dipping and scooping up the sauce and eggs.
8. Enjoy your homemade Shakshuka, a flavorful and satisfying dish that's perfect for breakfast, brunch, or even dinner!

Note: Shakshuka is highly customizable, so feel free to adjust the seasonings and add additional ingredients such as diced tomatoes, spinach, or olives according to your preferences.

Turkish Breakfast Platter (Turkey)

Ingredients:

- Simit (Turkish sesame bread) or crusty bread
- Soft white cheese (such as feta, beyaz peynir, or labneh)
- Hard cheese (such as kaşar or aged kashkaval)
- Olives (green or black, marinated or plain)
- Tomatoes, sliced
- Cucumbers, sliced
- Boiled eggs, sliced or halved
- Sucuk (Turkish spicy sausage), sliced and fried (optional)
- Pastırma (Turkish cured beef), thinly sliced (optional)
- Honey or jam
- Fresh herbs (such as parsley, dill, or cilantro), for garnish
- Turkish tea or coffee, to accompany the meal

Instructions:

1. Arrange the simit or crusty bread on a large serving platter as the centerpiece of the breakfast spread.
2. Place small bowls or plates of soft white cheese, hard cheese, and olives around the platter, allowing guests to help themselves.
3. Arrange the sliced tomatoes, cucumbers, and boiled eggs on the platter, either in separate sections or interspersed with the other ingredients.
4. If using, add slices of fried sucuk (Turkish sausage) and thinly sliced pastırma (cured beef) to the platter.
5. Serve honey or jam in small bowls or jars alongside the platter for spreading on bread or cheese.
6. Garnish the platter with fresh herbs for a pop of color and extra flavor.
7. Serve Turkish tea or coffee in traditional glasses or cups to accompany the meal.

8. Enjoy your Turkish breakfast platter with family and friends, savoring the variety of flavors and textures that make up this delightful morning meal!

Note: Turkish breakfast is often enjoyed as a leisurely affair, with friends and family gathered around the table to enjoy each other's company and the delicious spread of food. Feel free to customize your breakfast platter with additional ingredients such as sliced peppers, green onions, or Turkish-style omelets (menemen) according to your preferences.

Congee (China)

Ingredients:

- 1/2 cup long-grain white rice
- 6 cups water or chicken broth
- Salt, to taste
- Optional toppings: sliced green onions, chopped cilantro, sliced ginger, fried shallots, shredded chicken, sliced boiled eggs, tofu, cooked seafood, preserved vegetables, soy sauce, sesame oil, chili oil, etc.

Instructions:

1. Rinse the rice under cold water until the water runs clear. Drain well.
2. In a large pot, combine the rinsed rice and water or chicken broth. Bring to a boil over high heat.
3. Once boiling, reduce the heat to low and simmer the rice, partially covered, stirring occasionally to prevent sticking, for about 1 to 1 1/2 hours, or until the rice has broken down and the congee has reached your desired consistency. If the congee becomes too thick, you can add more water or broth to thin it out.
4. Season the congee with salt to taste.
5. Ladle the congee into serving bowls and garnish with your choice of toppings, such as sliced green onions, chopped cilantro, sliced ginger, fried shallots,

shredded chicken, sliced boiled eggs, tofu, cooked seafood, preserved vegetables, soy sauce, sesame oil, chili oil, etc.
6. Serve the congee hot, and enjoy this comforting and nourishing Chinese breakfast dish!

Note: Congee can be customized with a wide variety of toppings according to your preferences and dietary restrictions. Feel free to get creative and experiment with different flavor combinations to create your own unique bowl of congee. Additionally, leftover congee can be refrigerated and reheated later, although it may thicken further as it cools, so you may need to add more water or broth when reheating.

Dim Sum (China)

Ingredients:

For the filling:

- 1/2 pound ground pork
- 1/4 cup finely chopped shrimp
- 2 tablespoons finely chopped water chestnuts
- 2 tablespoons finely chopped green onions
- 1 tablespoon soy sauce
- 1 tablespoon oyster sauce
- 1 tablespoon sesame oil
- 1 teaspoon sugar
- 1/2 teaspoon salt
- 1/4 teaspoon white pepper

For the wrappers:

- Round dumpling wrappers (also called wonton wrappers), about 30 pieces

For garnish (optional):

- Peas, carrot slices, or other vegetables for garnish

Instructions:

1. In a large mixing bowl, combine the ground pork, chopped shrimp, water chestnuts, green onions, soy sauce, oyster sauce, sesame oil, sugar, salt, and white pepper. Mix well until all ingredients are evenly incorporated.
2. Take a dumpling wrapper and place about 1 tablespoon of the filling in the center.
3. Gather the edges of the wrapper around the filling, leaving the top open, and use your fingers to pleat and shape the wrapper around the filling. Press the filling down lightly as you shape the dumpling to flatten the bottom.
4. Repeat with the remaining wrappers and filling until all the filling is used.
5. Optional: Garnish each dumpling with a pea, carrot slice, or other vegetable for decoration.
6. Steam the siu mai dumplings in a bamboo steamer lined with parchment paper or cabbage leaves, making sure to leave some space between each dumpling to prevent them from sticking together. Steam for about 8-10 minutes, or until the filling is cooked through and the wrappers are translucent and tender.
7. Carefully remove the steamed siu mai dumplings from the steamer and transfer them to a serving plate.
8. Serve the siu mai dumplings hot, accompanied by soy sauce, chili oil, or other dipping sauces of your choice.
9. Enjoy your homemade siu mai dumplings as a delicious and satisfying dim sum treat!

Feel free to adjust the filling ingredients according to your preferences, such as adding more vegetables or using different seasonings. You can also experiment with different shapes and sizes for your dumplings.

Bánh Mì (Vietnam)

Ingredients:

For the baguette:

- 4 Vietnamese-style baguettes (or substitute with small French baguettes)
- Butter or mayonnaise, for spreading

For the protein (choose one or a combination):

- Grilled or pan-fried pork slices
- Grilled or shredded chicken
- Grilled or marinated tofu
- Vietnamese-style meatballs (xíu mại)
- Vietnamese-style cold cuts (thịt nguội)

For the pickled vegetables:

- 1 large carrot, julienned
- 1 medium daikon radish, julienned
- 1/2 cup rice vinegar
- 1/4 cup sugar
- 1 teaspoon salt

For the sandwich assembly:

- Cucumber, thinly sliced
- Fresh cilantro sprigs
- Fresh jalapeño or Thai chili slices (optional)
- Soy sauce or hoisin sauce (optional)
- Sriracha or chili garlic sauce (optional)

Instructions:

1. Prepare the pickled vegetables: In a bowl, mix together the rice vinegar, sugar, and salt until the sugar and salt are dissolved. Add the julienned carrot and daikon radish to the vinegar mixture, making sure they are fully submerged. Let marinate for at least 30 minutes, or ideally overnight in the refrigerator.

2. Preheat your oven to 350°F (175°C). Slice the baguettes lengthwise, but not all the way through, leaving one side intact. Spread butter or mayonnaise inside the baguettes.
3. If using, warm the protein filling(s) in a skillet or grill until heated through.
4. Remove the pickled vegetables from the marinade and drain off any excess liquid.
5. Assemble the bánh mì sandwiches: Layer the sliced protein filling(s) on the bottom half of each baguette, followed by the pickled vegetables, sliced cucumber, cilantro sprigs, and jalapeño or Thai chili slices (if using). Drizzle with soy sauce or hoisin sauce, and add a dollop of sriracha or chili garlic sauce for extra heat, if desired.
6. Close the baguettes and wrap each sandwich tightly in parchment paper or foil.
7. Place the wrapped sandwiches on a baking sheet and bake in the preheated oven for about 10-15 minutes, or until the baguettes are warmed through and the fillings are heated.
8. Remove the sandwiches from the oven and let them cool slightly before unwrapping and serving.
9. Serve the bánh mì sandwiches warm, and enjoy this delicious fusion of flavors and textures!

Note: Bánh mì sandwiches are highly customizable, so feel free to experiment with different protein fillings, toppings, and condiments according to your preferences. Traditional bánh mì often includes a combination of savory, sweet, tangy, and spicy flavors for a balanced and satisfying taste experience.

Pho (Vietnam)

Ingredients:

For the broth:

- 2 onions, halved
- 1 piece of ginger (about 3 inches), halved lengthwise
- 5-6 pounds beef bones (such as oxtail, marrow, or knuckle bones)
- 1 cinnamon stick

- 3 star anise
- 4-5 cloves
- 1 cardamom pod
- 1 teaspoon coriander seeds
- 1 tablespoon salt
- 1 tablespoon sugar
- 1/4 cup fish sauce
- Water

For the soup:

- 1 pound beef sirloin, thinly sliced
- 1 pound rice noodles (banh pho)
- 1 onion, thinly sliced
- 4-5 green onions, thinly sliced
- Fresh cilantro sprigs
- Bean sprouts
- Thai basil leaves
- Lime wedges
- Hoisin sauce
- Sriracha or chili sauce

Instructions:

1. Char the onions and ginger: Place the halved onions and ginger on a baking sheet and broil in the oven until charred, about 10-15 minutes. Alternatively, you can char them over an open flame on a gas stove.
2. Parboil the beef bones: Place the beef bones in a large pot and cover with cold water. Bring to a boil over high heat and let boil vigorously for 10 minutes. Drain the bones and rinse them under cold water to remove any impurities.
3. Make the broth: In a large stockpot, add the parboiled beef bones, charred onions, charred ginger, cinnamon stick, star anise, cloves, cardamom pod, coriander seeds, salt, sugar, and fish sauce. Cover with water, about 4-5 quarts, and bring to a boil over high heat. Skim off any foam that rises to the surface. Reduce the heat to low and let simmer gently, uncovered, for at least 4 hours, ideally 6-8 hours, to develop the flavors.

4. Strain the broth: After simmering, strain the broth through a fine-mesh sieve or cheesecloth to remove the solids. Discard the solids and return the broth to the pot. Taste and adjust seasoning, adding more salt, sugar, or fish sauce if needed.
5. Prepare the toppings: Soak the rice noodles in hot water for about 20-30 minutes, or according to package instructions, until softened. Thinly slice the onion and green onions. Prepare the bean sprouts, cilantro sprigs, Thai basil leaves, lime wedges, hoisin sauce, and sriracha or chili sauce for serving.
6. Assemble the pho bowls: Divide the softened rice noodles among serving bowls. Top with slices of raw beef sirloin, thinly sliced onion, and green onion. Ladle the hot broth over the noodles and beef, ensuring that the beef cooks in the hot broth.
7. Serve the pho: Serve the pho hot, accompanied by the prepared toppings and condiments. Diners can customize their pho bowls with bean sprouts, herbs, lime juice, hoisin sauce, and sriracha or chili sauce according to their taste preferences.
8. Enjoy your homemade beef pho, a comforting and flavorful Vietnamese noodle soup!

Note: Pho is a versatile dish, and you can adjust the ingredients and toppings according to your preferences. For a quicker version, you can use store-bought beef broth and add aromatics and spices to enhance the flavor. Additionally, you can substitute beef with chicken to make chicken pho (phở gà).

Kimchi Fried Rice (Korea)

Ingredients:

- 2 cups cooked rice (preferably day-old rice)
- 1 cup kimchi, chopped
- 2 tablespoons kimchi juice (from the jar)
- 2 tablespoons vegetable oil
- 1 small onion, finely chopped
- 2 cloves garlic, minced
- 1 carrot, diced
- 1/2 cup frozen peas

- 2 green onions, thinly sliced
- 2 eggs
- 2 tablespoons soy sauce
- 1 tablespoon sesame oil
- 1 teaspoon sugar (optional)
- Salt and pepper, to taste
- Toasted sesame seeds, for garnish (optional)

Instructions:

1. Heat vegetable oil in a large skillet or wok over medium heat. Add chopped onion and minced garlic, and cook until softened and fragrant, about 2-3 minutes.
2. Add diced carrot and cook for another 2-3 minutes, until slightly softened.
3. Add chopped kimchi to the skillet and stir-fry for 3-4 minutes, until heated through and slightly caramelized.
4. Push the kimchi mixture to one side of the skillet and crack the eggs into the empty space. Scramble the eggs until fully cooked, then mix them with the kimchi mixture.
5. Add cooked rice to the skillet, breaking up any clumps with a spatula. Stir-fry everything together for a few minutes, until the rice is well-coated with the kimchi mixture.
6. Stir in frozen peas, sliced green onions, soy sauce, kimchi juice, sesame oil, and sugar (if using). Season with salt and pepper to taste.
7. Continue to stir-fry for another 2-3 minutes, until the peas are heated through and the flavors are well combined.
8. Taste and adjust seasoning, if needed. If the fried rice is too dry, you can add a splash of water or more kimchi juice.
9. Remove the skillet from heat and transfer the kimchi fried rice to serving plates.
10. Garnish with toasted sesame seeds, if desired, and serve hot.
11. Enjoy your homemade kimchi fried rice as a delicious and satisfying meal!

Note: Feel free to customize your kimchi fried rice by adding other ingredients such as diced tofu, cooked shrimp, or sliced pork belly. You can also adjust the amount of kimchi and kimchi juice according to your taste preferences.

Onigiri (Japan)

Ingredients:

- 2 cups Japanese short-grain rice (sushi rice)
- 2 1/2 cups water
- 1/4 cup rice vinegar
- 2 tablespoons sugar
- 1 teaspoon salt
- Filling options: cooked salmon, tuna, pickled plum (umeboshi), cooked shrimp, cooked vegetables, etc.
- Optional garnishes: nori (seaweed) strips, sesame seeds, furikake (Japanese rice seasoning), etc.

Instructions:

1. Rinse the rice: Place the rice in a fine-mesh sieve and rinse it under cold water until the water runs clear. Drain well.
2. Cook the rice: In a rice cooker or a medium saucepan, combine the rinsed rice and water. Cook according to the manufacturer's instructions for your rice cooker or bring to a boil, then reduce the heat to low, cover, and simmer for about 15-20 minutes, or until the rice is cooked and tender.
3. Prepare the seasoning: In a small saucepan, combine the rice vinegar, sugar, and salt. Heat over low heat, stirring until the sugar and salt are dissolved. Remove from heat and let cool slightly.
4. Season the rice: Transfer the cooked rice to a large bowl and gently fold in the seasoned vinegar mixture using a rice paddle or spatula. Be careful not to mash the rice. Allow the seasoned rice to cool to room temperature.
5. Prepare the fillings: If using fillings such as cooked salmon, tuna, shrimp, or vegetables, make sure they are cooked and seasoned to your liking. You can also use pickled plum (umeboshi) as a traditional filling.
6. Form the onigiri: Wet your hands with water to prevent the rice from sticking. Take a small handful of seasoned rice and place it in the palm of your hand. Flatten the rice slightly and make an indentation in the center. Place a small amount of filling in the indentation, then cover it with more rice. Shape the rice into a triangular or cylindrical shape, pressing firmly to compact it.
7. Optional garnishes: If using nori strips, wrap them around the onigiri to cover the bottom half or top half of the rice ball. Alternatively, you can sprinkle sesame seeds or furikake over the onigiri for extra flavor and texture.

8. Repeat the process with the remaining rice and fillings until all the onigiri are formed.
9. Serve the onigiri at room temperature or chilled, and enjoy them as a tasty and portable snack!

Note: Onigiri can be stored in an airtight container at room temperature for a few hours or refrigerated for longer storage. They are best enjoyed within a day or two of making them. Feel free to get creative with fillings and shapes to make your own unique onigiri creations.

Miso Soup (Japan)

Ingredients:

- 4 cups water
- 2 tablespoons dashi granules (or kombu and bonito flakes for homemade dashi)
- 3-4 tablespoons miso paste (white or red)
- 1/2 block (about 4 ounces) firm tofu, cut into small cubes
- 2 green onions, thinly sliced
- 1 sheet dried seaweed (nori), cut into small pieces (optional)
- Optional additional ingredients: sliced mushrooms, spinach, wakame seaweed, cooked shrimp, clams, etc.

Instructions:

1. Prepare the dashi: In a medium saucepan, bring the water to a simmer. If using dashi granules, dissolve them in the simmering water. If making homemade dashi, add a piece of kombu (dried kelp) to the water and let it simmer for about 5 minutes, then remove the kombu and add a handful of bonito flakes (dried fish flakes). Let the bonito flakes steep for 1-2 minutes, then strain the dashi through a fine-mesh sieve or cheesecloth to remove any solids.
2. Add the tofu: Once the dashi is prepared, add the cubed tofu to the saucepan and let it simmer for a few minutes until heated through.

3. Dissolve the miso paste: In a small bowl, place the miso paste. Add a small amount of the hot dashi broth to the miso paste and whisk until smooth and well combined. This step helps to dissolve the miso paste evenly into the soup without forming lumps.
4. Add the miso mixture to the soup: Gradually pour the dissolved miso paste into the saucepan with the simmering dashi and tofu, stirring gently to combine. Be careful not to boil the miso soup once the miso paste has been added, as boiling can destroy the flavor of the miso.
5. Add additional ingredients: At this point, you can add any additional ingredients you like, such as sliced green onions, dried seaweed (nori), sliced mushrooms, spinach, wakame seaweed, cooked shrimp, clams, etc. Let the soup simmer for another minute or two until all the ingredients are heated through.
6. Taste and adjust seasoning: Taste the miso soup and adjust the seasoning if needed. You can add more miso paste for a stronger flavor, or dilute the soup with more water if it's too salty.
7. Serve the miso soup hot: Ladle the miso soup into individual bowls and garnish with additional sliced green onions or seaweed, if desired. Serve hot and enjoy as a comforting and nourishing Japanese soup!

Note: Miso soup is highly customizable, so feel free to experiment with different combinations of ingredients and adjust the proportions of miso paste and dashi to suit your taste preferences. You can also add cooked noodles or rice for a heartier meal.

Aussie Breakfast Pie (Australia)

Ingredients:

- 1 package of store-bought pie crusts (or homemade pie crust)
- 6 eggs
- 6 slices of bacon, chopped
- 4 breakfast sausages, casings removed
- 1 small onion, finely chopped
- 1 bell pepper (capsicum), diced
- 1 cup diced mushrooms
- 1 cup shredded cheddar cheese
- Salt and pepper, to taste

- Olive oil, for cooking
- Optional: chopped fresh herbs like parsley or chives, for garnish

Instructions:

1. Preheat your oven to 375°F (190°C).
2. In a skillet, cook the chopped bacon over medium heat until crispy. Remove from the skillet and set aside. Drain excess fat from the skillet.
3. In the same skillet, add the breakfast sausages (removed from casings) and cook, breaking them apart with a spatula, until browned and cooked through. Remove from the skillet and set aside.
4. In the same skillet, add a little olive oil if needed, then add the chopped onion, diced bell pepper, and diced mushrooms. Cook until softened, about 5-7 minutes. Season with salt and pepper to taste.
5. Roll out the pie crusts and cut them into circles to fit into the wells of a muffin tin, or use mini pie tins. Press the pie crusts into the wells, making sure to leave some overhang.
6. Divide the cooked bacon, sausage, and vegetable mixture among the pie crusts, distributing them evenly.
7. Crack an egg into each pie crust on top of the filling. Be careful not to break the yolk.
8. Sprinkle shredded cheddar cheese over each pie.
9. Fold the overhanging edges of the pie crust over the filling, leaving the center of the egg exposed.
10. Bake the pies in the preheated oven for 15-20 minutes, or until the crust is golden brown and the egg whites are set but the yolks are still runny. If you prefer firmer yolks, bake for a few minutes longer.
11. Remove the pies from the oven and let them cool slightly before serving.
12. Garnish with chopped fresh herbs if desired, and enjoy your Aussie Breakfast Pies hot or at room temperature!

These Aussie Breakfast Pies are perfect for a weekend brunch or breakfast on the go.

They're portable, delicious, and packed with all your favorite breakfast flavors.

Vegemite on Toast (Australia)

Ingredients:

- Slices of bread (white, whole wheat, or your preferred type)
- Butter or margarine
- Vegemite

Instructions:

1. Toast the bread slices until they are golden brown and crispy.
2. Spread a thin layer of butter or margarine on each slice of toast while it's still warm. This helps the Vegemite spread more easily and adds a delicious richness to the toast.
3. Using a knife, spread a thin layer of Vegemite onto the buttered toast. Start with a small amount and add more to taste, as Vegemite has a strong and salty flavor.
4. Spread the Vegemite evenly over the entire surface of the toast, making sure to cover it from edge to edge.
5. Serve the Vegemite on toast immediately while it's still warm and the butter is melted. Enjoy it as a quick and satisfying breakfast or snack!

Note: Vegemite on toast is typically enjoyed with a cup of tea or coffee, and it's a popular choice for breakfast or as a light meal throughout the day. You can also get creative with your Vegemite toast by adding toppings like avocado slices, tomato slices, or cheese for extra flavor and texture. Adjust the amount of Vegemite according to your personal taste preferences, as it can be quite strong for some palates.

Lamingtons (Australia)

Ingredients:

For the sponge cake:

- 1 3/4 cups all-purpose flour

- 1 teaspoon baking powder
- 1/4 teaspoon salt
- 1/2 cup unsalted butter, softened
- 3/4 cup granulated sugar
- 2 large eggs
- 1 teaspoon vanilla extract
- 1/2 cup milk

For the chocolate icing:

- 3 cups powdered sugar (icing sugar)
- 1/4 cup unsweetened cocoa powder
- 2 tablespoons unsalted butter, melted
- 1/2 cup milk
- 1 teaspoon vanilla extract

For assembling:

- 2 cups desiccated coconut

Instructions:

1. Preheat your oven to 350°F (180°C). Grease and flour a 9x13-inch baking pan or line it with parchment paper.
2. In a medium bowl, whisk together the flour, baking powder, and salt. Set aside.
3. In a large mixing bowl, cream together the softened butter and granulated sugar until light and fluffy.
4. Beat in the eggs, one at a time, until well combined. Add the vanilla extract and mix until smooth.
5. Gradually add the flour mixture to the wet ingredients, alternating with the milk, beginning and ending with the flour mixture. Mix until just combined, being careful not to overmix.
6. Pour the batter into the prepared baking pan and spread it out evenly.
7. Bake in the preheated oven for 25-30 minutes, or until a toothpick inserted into the center comes out clean and the cake is golden brown.
8. Remove the cake from the oven and let it cool completely in the pan.

9. Once the cake is cool, cut it into squares or rectangles, about 2x2 inches in size.
10. Place the desiccated coconut in a shallow dish.
11. To make the chocolate icing, sift the powdered sugar and cocoa powder into a medium bowl. Add the melted butter, milk, and vanilla extract, and whisk until smooth.
12. Dip each cake square into the chocolate icing, coating it completely, then roll it in the desiccated coconut until evenly coated.
13. Place the coated lamingtons on a wire rack to set. Repeat the dipping and rolling process with the remaining cake squares and icing.
14. Once the icing has set, serve the lamingtons and enjoy!

Note: Lamingtons can be stored in an airtight container at room temperature for up to 3 days. They can also be frozen for longer storage.

Kiwi Fruit Salad (New Zealand)

Ingredients:

- 4-5 ripe kiwifruits, peeled and sliced
- 1 cup strawberries, hulled and sliced
- 1 cup fresh pineapple, diced
- 1 cup green grapes, halved
- 1 banana, sliced
- Juice of 1 lime or lemon
- 2 tablespoons honey or maple syrup (optional)
- Fresh mint leaves, for garnish (optional)

Instructions:

1. In a large mixing bowl, combine the sliced kiwifruits, strawberries, pineapple, grapes, and banana.
2. Squeeze the lime or lemon juice over the fruit salad. This not only adds a refreshing citrus flavor but also helps to prevent the fruits from browning.

3. If desired, drizzle honey or maple syrup over the fruit salad for added sweetness. This step is optional, depending on the sweetness of the fruits and your personal preference.
4. Gently toss the fruit salad until all the fruits are evenly coated with the lime or lemon juice and honey or maple syrup, if using.
5. Transfer the fruit salad to a serving dish or individual bowls.
6. Garnish the fruit salad with fresh mint leaves for a pop of color and additional freshness.
7. Serve the Kiwi Fruit Salad immediately as a refreshing and healthy snack, side dish, or dessert.

This Kiwi Fruit Salad is not only delicious but also packed with vitamins, minerals, and antioxidants from the assortment of fresh fruits. Feel free to customize the fruit selection according to your preferences and what's in season. Enjoy the vibrant flavors of New Zealand's kiwifruit in this delightful salad!

Canadian Bacon and Eggs (Canada)

Ingredients:

- Canadian bacon slices (about 2-3 slices per person)
- Eggs (1-2 eggs per person)
- Butter or cooking oil
- Salt and pepper, to taste
- Optional garnishes: chopped fresh herbs, grated cheese, sliced avocado, salsa, etc.

Instructions:

1. Heat a skillet or frying pan over medium heat. Add a small amount of butter or cooking oil to the pan, then add the Canadian bacon slices in a single layer.
2. Cook the Canadian bacon for 2-3 minutes on each side, or until golden brown and heated through. Remove from the pan and set aside, keeping warm.

3. In the same pan, crack the eggs and cook them to your desired doneness. You can fry them sunny-side up, over-easy, scrambled, poached, or however you prefer.
4. Season the eggs with salt and pepper to taste while cooking.
5. Once the eggs are cooked, transfer them to serving plates alongside the cooked Canadian bacon.
6. Optionally, garnish the Canadian bacon and eggs with chopped fresh herbs, grated cheese, sliced avocado, salsa, or any other toppings of your choice.
7. Serve the Canadian bacon and eggs hot, accompanied by toast, English muffins, or your favorite breakfast sides.
8. Enjoy this classic Canadian breakfast dish as a hearty and satisfying way to start your day!

Canadian bacon and eggs is a versatile dish that can be customized with different cooking methods and toppings to suit your taste preferences. Whether you enjoy it for breakfast, brunch, or even dinner, it's sure to be a comforting and delicious meal.

BeaverTails (Canada)

Ingredients:

For the dough:

- 1 cup warm water (about 110°F/45°C)
- 2 1/4 teaspoons active dry yeast
- 1/4 cup granulated sugar
- 1/2 teaspoon salt
- 1/4 cup unsalted butter, melted
- 1 large egg
- 4 cups all-purpose flour, plus more for dusting

For frying:

- Vegetable oil, for frying

For topping:

- Cinnamon sugar (1 cup granulated sugar mixed with 2 tablespoons ground cinnamon)
- Maple syrup
- Nutella
- Sliced bananas
- Crushed Oreos
- Chopped nuts
- Whipped cream
- Your favorite toppings

Instructions:

1. In a small bowl, combine warm water, active dry yeast, and a pinch of sugar. Let it sit for about 5-10 minutes, until the mixture becomes frothy.
2. In a large mixing bowl, combine the frothy yeast mixture with sugar, salt, melted butter, and egg. Mix well.
3. Gradually add the flour, stirring until a soft dough forms.
4. Transfer the dough to a floured surface and knead for about 5-7 minutes, until the dough is smooth and elastic.
5. Place the dough in a greased bowl, cover with a clean kitchen towel or plastic wrap, and let it rise in a warm place for about 1-2 hours, or until doubled in size.
6. Once the dough has risen, punch it down and divide it into 8 equal portions.
7. Roll each portion of dough into an oval shape, resembling a beaver's tail. Make sure the dough is about 1/4 inch thick.
8. Heat vegetable oil in a deep fryer or large pot to 375°F (190°C).
9. Carefully place one piece of dough into the hot oil and fry for about 1-2 minutes on each side, until golden brown and puffed up. Use a slotted spoon to flip the dough halfway through frying.
10. Remove the fried dough from the oil and drain on paper towels to remove excess oil.
11. While still warm, generously sprinkle the BeaverTail with cinnamon sugar, or spread with Nutella, maple syrup, or any other toppings of your choice.
12. Repeat the frying process with the remaining pieces of dough.
13. Serve the BeaverTails warm and enjoy them as a delicious Canadian treat!

BeaverTails are best enjoyed fresh and warm, but they can also be stored in an airtight container at room temperature for up to 1-2 days. Simply reheat them in the oven or toaster oven before serving, if desired.

Poutine (Canada)

Ingredients:

For the fries:

- 4 large russet potatoes, peeled and cut into fries
- Vegetable oil, for frying
- Salt, to taste

For the gravy:

- 2 tablespoons unsalted butter
- 2 tablespoons all-purpose flour
- 2 cups beef broth (or chicken broth)
- Salt and pepper, to taste

For assembling:

- 2 cups cheese curds, preferably fresh and squeaky

Instructions:

1. Prepare the fries: Rinse the cut potatoes under cold water to remove excess starch. Pat them dry with paper towels.
2. Heat vegetable oil in a deep fryer or large pot to 325°F (160°C). Fry the potatoes in batches until golden brown and crispy, about 5-7 minutes per batch. Remove from the oil and drain on paper towels. Season with salt while still hot.

3. Make the gravy: In a medium saucepan, melt the butter over medium heat. Add the flour and cook, stirring constantly, for 1-2 minutes to make a roux.
4. Gradually whisk in the beef broth, stirring constantly to prevent lumps from forming. Bring the gravy to a simmer and cook for 5-7 minutes, or until thickened. Season with salt and pepper to taste.
5. Assemble the poutine: Place a serving of hot fries in a bowl or on a plate. Sprinkle a generous amount of cheese curds over the fries. Pour hot gravy over the fries and cheese curds, allowing the cheese to melt slightly from the heat of the gravy.
6. Serve the poutine immediately, while hot and gooey, and enjoy the delicious combination of crispy fries, squeaky cheese curds, and savory gravy!

Note: Poutine is a versatile dish, and you can customize it to your liking by adding additional toppings such as cooked bacon, pulled pork, caramelized onions, mushrooms, or green onions. You can also experiment with different types of cheese curds or gravy variations. Enjoy this iconic Canadian comfort food as a hearty snack, appetizer, or indulgent meal!

Smørrebrød (Denmark)

Ingredients:

- Dense rye bread (or another hearty bread of your choice)
- Butter or mayonnaise
- Assorted toppings (see below for suggestions)
- Garnishes such as fresh herbs, sliced vegetables, or pickles

Instructions:

1. Start by slicing the dense rye bread into thick slices. You can lightly toast the bread if desired, but it's traditionally served untoasted.

2. Spread a thin layer of butter or mayonnaise on each slice of bread. This helps to add flavor and also acts as a barrier to prevent the bread from becoming soggy from the toppings.
3. Choose your toppings. Smørrebrød can be topped with a wide variety of ingredients, including cold cuts, cured fish, cheeses, spreads, and vegetables. Here are some traditional topping ideas:
- Sliced roast beef or pork with remoulade (a Danish condiment similar to tartar sauce) and crispy fried onions
- Smoked salmon with cream cheese, fresh dill, and lemon wedges
- Pickled herring with onions, capers, and a dollop of sour cream
- Sliced hard-boiled eggs with mayonnaise, shrimp, and dill
- Sliced cucumber with cream cheese, radishes, and chives
- Liver pâté with bacon, pickles, and red onion rings
- Danish blue cheese with sliced apples, walnuts, and honey
4. Arrange your chosen toppings on the buttered bread slices, making sure to spread them evenly and create an attractive presentation.
5. Garnish the Smørrebrød with fresh herbs, sliced vegetables, or pickles for added flavor and visual appeal.
6. Serve the Smørrebrød immediately as an elegant and delicious open-faced sandwich. It's often enjoyed as a light lunch or as part of a festive smorgasbord (a traditional Scandinavian buffet).

Feel free to get creative and experiment with different combinations of toppings to suit your taste preferences. Smørrebrød is highly customizable, and there are endless possibilities for delicious flavor combinations. Enjoy this Danish culinary tradition at home with friends and family!

Kedgeree (India)

Ingredients:

- 1 cup long-grain rice
- 2 cups water
- 1/2 teaspoon salt
- 1 tablespoon vegetable oil or ghee

- 1 onion, finely chopped
- 2 cloves garlic, minced
- 1 tablespoon curry powder
- 1 teaspoon ground turmeric
- 1/2 teaspoon ground cumin
- 1/2 teaspoon ground coriander
- 1/4 teaspoon cayenne pepper (optional, for heat)
- 1 cup cooked flaked fish (traditionally smoked haddock, but you can use any flaky white fish such as cod or salmon)
- 2 hard-boiled eggs, chopped
- 1/4 cup chopped fresh parsley or cilantro (coriander leaves), plus extra for garnish
- Salt and pepper, to taste
- Lemon wedges, for serving

Instructions:

1. Rinse the rice under cold water until the water runs clear. In a saucepan, combine the rinsed rice, water, and salt. Bring to a boil over high heat, then reduce the heat to low, cover, and simmer for 15-20 minutes, or until the rice is cooked and the water is absorbed. Remove from heat and let it sit, covered, for 5 minutes.
2. While the rice is cooking, heat the vegetable oil or ghee in a large skillet over medium heat. Add the chopped onion and cook, stirring occasionally, until softened and lightly browned, about 5-7 minutes. Add the minced garlic and cook for another 1-2 minutes, until fragrant.
3. Stir in the curry powder, ground turmeric, ground cumin, ground coriander, and cayenne pepper (if using). Cook, stirring constantly, for 1-2 minutes, until the spices are toasted and fragrant.
4. Add the cooked flaked fish to the skillet and stir to combine with the spice mixture. Cook for 2-3 minutes, until the fish is heated through.
5. Add the cooked rice to the skillet and stir gently to combine with the fish and spices. Cook for another 2-3 minutes, until everything is well mixed and heated through.
6. Remove the skillet from heat and stir in the chopped hard-boiled eggs and chopped fresh parsley or cilantro. Season with salt and pepper to taste.
7. Transfer the kedgeree to a serving dish and garnish with additional chopped parsley or cilantro. Serve hot, with lemon wedges on the side for squeezing over the kedgeree.

8. Enjoy your homemade kedgeree as a comforting and flavorful meal, perfect for breakfast, brunch, or dinner!

Note: Kedgeree is a versatile dish, and you can adjust the ingredients and spices according to your taste preferences. Feel free to add extra vegetables such as peas, carrots, or bell peppers, or customize the spice level to your liking by adding more or less cayenne pepper.

Masala Dosa (India)

Ingredients:

For the dosa batter:

- 1 cup parboiled rice (also known as idli rice)
- 1/4 cup white rice
- 1/2 cup split black lentils (urad dal)
- 1/2 teaspoon fenugreek seeds (methi seeds)
- Water, as needed
- Salt, to taste

For the potato filling (masala):

- 3-4 large potatoes, boiled, peeled, and mashed
- 1 onion, finely chopped
- 1-2 green chilies, finely chopped
- 1 teaspoon mustard seeds
- 1 teaspoon cumin seeds
- 1/2 teaspoon turmeric powder
- 1/2 teaspoon red chili powder (optional, for heat)
- A handful of curry leaves
- Salt, to taste
- 2 tablespoons vegetable oil

For serving:

- Coconut chutney
- Sambar

Instructions:

1. Prepare the dosa batter:
   - Rinse the parboiled rice, white rice, split black lentils, and fenugreek seeds together under cold water until the water runs clear. Soak them in water for at least 4-6 hours or overnight.
   - Drain the soaked rice and lentils and transfer them to a blender. Add water as needed and blend until you get a smooth batter with a pourable consistency. The batter should be slightly thick but still spreadable. Add salt to taste and mix well. Transfer the batter to a large bowl and let it ferment in a warm place for 8-12 hours or until it doubles in volume.
2. Prepare the potato filling (masala):
   - Heat vegetable oil in a skillet or frying pan over medium heat. Add mustard seeds and cumin seeds and let them splutter.
   - Add chopped onion, green chilies, and curry leaves to the pan. Sauté until the onions turn translucent.
   - Add turmeric powder and red chili powder (if using) and mix well.
   - Add the mashed potatoes to the pan and stir to combine with the spices. Cook for 2-3 minutes, stirring occasionally, until the flavors are well combined. Season with salt to taste. Remove from heat and set aside.
3. Make the dosas:
   - Heat a non-stick skillet or dosa tawa over medium-high heat. Once hot, pour a ladleful of dosa batter onto the center of the skillet.
   - Using the back of the ladle, spread the batter in a circular motion to form a thin, even layer. Drizzle a little oil around the edges of the dosa.
   - Cook the dosa for 2-3 minutes, or until the bottom is golden brown and crispy. Flip the dosa using a spatula and cook for another 1-2 minutes on the other side.
   - Remove the dosa from the skillet and place it on a serving plate.
4. Assemble the masala dosas:
   - Place a spoonful of the prepared potato filling (masala) in the center of each dosa.
   - Fold the dosa over the filling to form a half-moon shape or roll it into a cylinder.
   - Serve hot masala dosas with coconut chutney and sambar on the side.

5. Enjoy your homemade masala dosas as a delicious and satisfying South Indian meal!

Note: You can adjust the spiciness of the potato filling (masala) by adding more or fewer green chilies and red chili powder according to your taste preferences. You can also add grated coconut, chopped cilantro, or other vegetables to the filling for extra flavor and texture.

Idli with Sambar (India)

Ingredients:

For the idli batter:

- 1 cup parboiled rice (also known as idli rice)
- 1/4 cup white rice
- 1/2 cup split black lentils (urad dal)
- 1/2 teaspoon fenugreek seeds (methi seeds)
- Water, as needed
- Salt, to taste

For the sambar:

- 1/2 cup pigeon peas (toor dal), washed and soaked for 30 minutes
- 2 cups mixed vegetables (such as carrots, potatoes, eggplant, tomatoes, drumsticks, etc.), chopped
- 1 onion, chopped
- 2 tomatoes, chopped
- 2-3 green chilies, slit lengthwise
- 1 tablespoon tamarind paste
- 1 teaspoon mustard seeds
- 1 teaspoon cumin seeds
- A pinch of asafoetida (hing)
- 1/2 teaspoon turmeric powder
- 1 tablespoon sambar powder (store-bought or homemade)
- A handful of curry leaves

- 2 tablespoons vegetable oil
- Salt, to taste

Instructions:

1. Prepare the idli batter:
    - Rinse the parboiled rice, white rice, split black lentils, and fenugreek seeds together under cold water until the water runs clear. Soak them in water for at least 4-6 hours or overnight.
    - Drain the soaked rice and lentils and transfer them to a blender. Add water as needed and blend until you get a smooth batter with a pourable consistency. The batter should be slightly thick but still spreadable. Add salt to taste and mix well. Transfer the batter to a large bowl and let it ferment in a warm place for 8-12 hours or until it doubles in volume.
2. Prepare the sambar:
    - Pressure cook the soaked pigeon peas (toor dal) with enough water until soft and mushy. Set aside.
    - In a large pot or saucepan, heat vegetable oil over medium heat. Add mustard seeds and cumin seeds and let them splutter.
    - Add chopped onions, green chilies, and curry leaves to the pot. Sauté until the onions turn translucent.
    - Add chopped tomatoes and cook until they turn soft and mushy.
    - Add the mixed vegetables, turmeric powder, sambar powder, and salt to the pot. Mix well to combine.
    - Add tamarind paste and cooked pigeon peas (toor dal) to the pot. Stir well and bring the sambar to a simmer. Cook for 15-20 minutes, or until the vegetables are tender and the flavors are well blended. Adjust the consistency of the sambar by adding more water if needed. Remove from heat and set aside.
3. Make the idlis:
    - Grease the idli plates or molds with a little oil.
    - Pour the fermented idli batter into the greased idli plates, filling each mold about 3/4 full.
    - Steam the idlis in a steamer or idli cooker for 10-12 minutes, or until they are cooked through and a toothpick inserted into the center comes out clean.
    - Remove the idli plates from the steamer and let them cool for a few minutes. Then, gently unmold the idlis using a spoon or butter knife.

4. Serve the idli with sambar:
    - Place 2-3 idlis on a serving plate. Pour a ladleful of hot sambar over the idlis.
    - Serve the idli with sambar hot, accompanied by coconut chutney or a dollop of ghee on the side.
5. Enjoy your homemade idli with sambar as a delicious and nutritious South Indian breakfast or snack!

Note: You can customize the vegetables used in the sambar according to your preferences and what's available. Feel free to add more or fewer green chilies and adjust the amount of sambar powder to suit your taste preferences.

Roti Canai (Malaysia)

Ingredients:

For the dough:

- 2 cups all-purpose flour
- 1/2 teaspoon salt
- 1 tablespoon sugar
- 1/4 cup condensed milk
- 1/4 cup water
- 2 tablespoons ghee or vegetable oil, plus extra for frying

For stretching and folding:

- Ghee or vegetable oil

Instructions:

1. In a large mixing bowl, combine the all-purpose flour, salt, and sugar. Mix well to combine.

2. Add the condensed milk, water, and ghee or vegetable oil to the dry ingredients. Mix until a dough forms.
3. Knead the dough on a lightly floured surface for about 5-10 minutes, or until it becomes smooth and elastic. If the dough is too sticky, add a little more flour. If it's too dry, add a little more water.
4. Divide the dough into small balls, about the size of a golf ball. Coat each ball of dough with a little ghee or vegetable oil to prevent them from drying out.
5. Place the balls of dough on a baking sheet or tray, cover with a clean kitchen towel or plastic wrap, and let them rest at room temperature for at least 4 hours, or preferably overnight. This allows the gluten to relax and makes the dough easier to stretch.
6. Once the dough has rested, take one ball of dough and flatten it with your hands on a lightly oiled surface. Using your fingertips, gently stretch and flatten the dough into a thin, translucent sheet. You can also use a rolling pin to roll out the dough if preferred.
7. Brush the surface of the stretched dough with a little ghee or vegetable oil.
8. Fold the dough into a rectangle or square by folding the edges towards the center, then folding the top and bottom edges over the center to form a parcel.
9. Heat a skillet or frying pan over medium heat. Once hot, carefully transfer the folded dough onto the skillet.
10. Cook the Roti Canai for 1-2 minutes on each side, or until golden brown and cooked through. Brush with more ghee or vegetable oil as needed while cooking.
11. Remove the Roti Canai from the skillet and serve hot with dhal (lentil curry) or your favorite curry.
12. Repeat the process with the remaining balls of dough.
13. Enjoy your homemade Roti Canai as a delicious and satisfying Malaysian flatbread!

Note: Roti Canai is best enjoyed fresh and hot off the skillet. You can also serve it with other accompaniments such as condensed milk, sugar, or curry sauces for dipping. Experiment with different fillings and toppings to create your own unique variations of Roti Canai.

Nasi Lemak (Malaysia)

Ingredients:

For the coconut rice:

- 2 cups jasmine rice
- 1 3/4 cups coconut milk
- 1 3/4 cups water
- 2 pandan leaves, tied into knots (optional)
- 1 teaspoon salt

For the sambal (spicy chili paste):

- 10-12 dried red chilies, soaked in hot water for 15-20 minutes
- 3 shallots, peeled
- 3 cloves garlic, peeled
- 1 inch piece of fresh ginger, peeled
- 2 tablespoons vegetable oil
- 1 tablespoon tamarind paste
- 2 tablespoons palm sugar or brown sugar
- Salt, to taste

For the accompaniments:

- Hard-boiled eggs, halved
- Cucumber slices
- Fried anchovies (ikan bilis)
- Roasted peanuts
- Slices of fresh cucumber and tomato
- Slices of fried or grilled chicken or fish (optional)

Instructions:

1. Prepare the coconut rice:
    - Rinse the jasmine rice under cold water until the water runs clear. Drain well.
    - In a rice cooker or a medium saucepan, combine the rinsed rice, coconut milk, water, pandan leaves (if using), and salt. Stir to combine.
    - Cook the rice according to the instructions of your rice cooker, or bring the mixture to a boil over medium heat in the saucepan. Once boiling, reduce

the heat to low, cover, and simmer for 15-20 minutes, or until the rice is cooked and the liquid is absorbed. Remove from heat and let it sit, covered, for 5 minutes. Fluff the rice with a fork before serving.
2. Prepare the sambal:
   - In a blender or food processor, combine the soaked dried red chilies, shallots, garlic, and ginger. Blend until you get a smooth paste. You can add a little water if needed to help with blending.
   - Heat vegetable oil in a skillet or frying pan over medium heat. Add the chili paste to the pan and sauté for 5-7 minutes, or until fragrant and the raw smell dissipates.
   - Stir in the tamarind paste and palm sugar or brown sugar. Cook for another 5-7 minutes, or until the sambal thickens slightly. Season with salt to taste. Remove from heat and set aside.
3. Prepare the accompaniments:
   - Fry the anchovies (ikan bilis) in a little oil until crispy. Drain on paper towels.
   - Roast the peanuts in a dry skillet over medium heat until lightly golden and fragrant.
   - Halve the hard-boiled eggs and slice the cucumber and tomato.
4. Serve the Nasi Lemak:
   - Spoon a serving of coconut rice onto each plate.
   - Serve with a spoonful of sambal, hard-boiled eggs, cucumber slices, tomato slices, fried anchovies, and roasted peanuts on the side.
   - Optionally, serve with slices of fried or grilled chicken or fish on the side.
   - Enjoy your homemade Nasi Lemak as a delicious and flavorful Malaysian meal!

Nasi Lemak is often enjoyed for breakfast or as a hearty meal any time of the day. It's a versatile dish, and you can customize the accompaniments and adjust the spiciness of the sambal according to your taste preferences.

Laksa (Singapore)

Ingredients:

For the laksa paste:

- 10-12 dried red chilies, soaked in hot water for 15-20 minutes
- 3 shallots, peeled
- 3 cloves garlic, peeled
- 1 inch piece of fresh ginger, peeled
- 2 stalks lemongrass, white part only, sliced
- 1 tablespoon shrimp paste (belacan)
- 1 tablespoon ground coriander
- 1 tablespoon ground turmeric
- 1 tablespoon ground cumin
- 1 teaspoon ground fennel seeds
- 1 teaspoon ground cinnamon
- 1/2 teaspoon ground cloves
- 1/2 teaspoon ground nutmeg
- 1/4 cup vegetable oil

For the laksa broth:

- 4 cups chicken or vegetable broth
- 2 cups coconut milk
- 2 kaffir lime leaves
- 1 tablespoon palm sugar or brown sugar
- 1 tablespoon fish sauce
- Salt, to taste

For the laksa:

- 200g rice vermicelli noodles, soaked in hot water until softened
- 200g shrimp, peeled and deveined
- 200g chicken breast, thinly sliced
- Tofu puffs, tofu slices, or fish cakes (optional)
- Hard-boiled eggs, halved (optional)
- Bean sprouts
- Fresh cilantro (coriander) leaves
- Lime wedges

Instructions:

1. Prepare the laksa paste:
   - In a blender or food processor, combine the soaked dried red chilies, shallots, garlic, ginger, lemongrass, shrimp paste, ground coriander, ground turmeric, ground cumin, ground fennel seeds, ground cinnamon, ground cloves, and ground nutmeg. Blend until you get a smooth paste.
2. Heat vegetable oil in a large pot over medium heat. Add the laksa paste to the pot and sauté for 5-7 minutes, or until fragrant.
3. Prepare the laksa broth:
   - Add chicken or vegetable broth to the pot with the laksa paste. Stir to combine.
   - Add coconut milk, kaffir lime leaves, palm sugar or brown sugar, fish sauce, and salt to taste. Bring the broth to a simmer and cook for 10-15 minutes, allowing the flavors to meld together. Taste and adjust seasoning if needed.
4. Cook the laksa ingredients:
   - Add shrimp and chicken slices to the simmering laksa broth. Cook for 3-5 minutes, or until the shrimp is pink and cooked through and the chicken is cooked.
   - If using tofu puffs, tofu slices, or fish cakes, add them to the broth and cook for another 2-3 minutes, or until heated through.
5. Assemble the laksa:
   - Divide the softened rice vermicelli noodles among serving bowls.
   - Ladle the hot laksa broth over the noodles, making sure to include shrimp, chicken, and other toppings.
   - Garnish the laksa with hard-boiled eggs (if using), bean sprouts, fresh cilantro leaves, and lime wedges.
6. Serve the laksa hot, with additional sambal chili paste on the side for those who prefer extra heat.
7. Enjoy your homemade Singaporean laksa as a flavorful and satisfying noodle soup!

Note: You can customize the laksa toppings according to your preferences. Feel free to add other ingredients such as sliced fish cakes, fried tofu, or sliced fish balls. Adjust the spiciness of the laksa paste by adding more or fewer dried red chilies.

Hainanese Chicken Rice (Singapore)Ingredients:

For the chicken:

1 whole chicken (about 3-4 pounds), preferably free-range

6 cups water

4 slices ginger

2 stalks scallions, cut into 2-inch pieces

Salt, to taste

For the rice:

2 cups jasmine rice

3 cups chicken broth (from poaching the chicken)

2 slices ginger

2 cloves garlic, minced

Salt, to taste

For the chili sauce:

4-6 red chili peppers, seeds removed and chopped

2 cloves garlic, minced

2 tablespoons ginger, minced

2 tablespoons lime juice

1 tablespoon chicken broth

1 tablespoon sesame oil

1 tablespoon soy sauce

Salt, to taste

For the ginger paste:

2 inches ginger, peeled and minced

2 cloves garlic, minced

1 tablespoon sesame oil

Salt, to taste

For garnish:

Fresh cilantro (coriander) leaves

Sliced cucumber

Instructions:

Prepare the chicken:

Rinse the chicken under cold water and pat dry with paper towels.

In a large pot, bring water to a boil. Add ginger slices, scallions, and a pinch of salt.

Carefully lower the whole chicken into the pot, breast side down. Return the water to a boil, then reduce the heat to low. Cover and simmer for 30-40 minutes, or until the chicken is cooked through.

Remove the chicken from the pot and immediately transfer it to a bowl of ice water to stop the cooking process. Let it cool completely, then remove the chicken from the water and set aside. Reserve the chicken broth for cooking the rice.

Prepare the rice:

Rinse the jasmine rice under cold water until the water runs clear. Drain well.

In a medium saucepan, heat a little oil over medium heat. Add minced garlic and ginger and sauté until fragrant.

Add the rinsed rice to the saucepan and stir to coat with the garlic and ginger.

Pour in the chicken broth (strained from poaching the chicken) and add a pinch of salt. Bring to a boil, then reduce the heat to low. Cover and simmer for 15-20 minutes, or until the rice is cooked and fluffy.

Prepare the chili sauce:

In a blender or food processor, combine chopped red chili peppers, minced garlic, minced ginger, lime juice, chicken broth, sesame oil, soy sauce, and a pinch of salt. Blend until smooth. Adjust seasoning to taste.

Prepare the ginger paste:

In a small bowl, mix together minced ginger, minced garlic, sesame oil, and a pinch of salt. Set aside.

Serve the Hainanese Chicken Rice:

Cut the poached chicken into serving pieces.

Serve the chicken alongside the fragrant rice, chili sauce, and ginger paste.

Garnish with fresh cilantro leaves and sliced cucumber.

Enjoy your homemade Hainanese Chicken Rice with all the condiments and flavors!

Hainanese Chicken Rice is often enjoyed with a bowl of clear chicken broth on the side. You can also serve it with additional soy sauce or dark soy sauce for dipping the chicken. Adjust the spiciness of the chili sauce according to your taste preferences.

Kaya Toast (Singapore)

Ingredients:

For the kaya (coconut and pandan jam):

- 4 large eggs
- 200g sugar
- 200ml coconut milk
- 4 pandan leaves, tied into knots
- 1/2 teaspoon salt

For assembling:

- Slices of white bread
- Butter or margarine
- Soft-boiled eggs (optional)
- Coffee or tea

Instructions:

1. Prepare the kaya:
    - In a heatproof bowl, whisk together the eggs and sugar until well combined.
    - In a saucepan, heat the coconut milk and pandan leaves over medium heat until it just begins to simmer. Remove from heat.
    - Slowly pour the hot coconut milk into the egg mixture, whisking constantly to combine.
    - Return the mixture to the saucepan and place over low heat. Cook, stirring constantly, until the mixture thickens to a custard-like consistency, about 20-30 minutes. Be careful not to let it boil.
    - Once thickened, remove the pandan leaves and stir in the salt. Allow the kaya to cool completely before using.
2. Toast the bread:
    - Toast slices of white bread until golden brown and crispy on both sides.

3. Assemble the Kaya Toast:
    - Spread a generous amount of butter or margarine on one side of each toasted bread slice.
    - Spread a thick layer of kaya (coconut and pandan jam) on top of the buttered side of one bread slice.
    - Place another bread slice, buttered side down, on top of the kaya to form a sandwich.
    - Repeat with the remaining bread slices and kaya.
4. Serve the Kaya Toast:
    - Cut the Kaya Toast into halves or quarters, if desired.
    - Serve with soft-boiled eggs on the side, if using.
    - Enjoy your homemade Kaya Toast with a cup of hot coffee or tea for a delicious and comforting breakfast or snack!

Kaya Toast is often enjoyed as part of a traditional Singaporean or Malaysian breakfast, alongside soft-boiled eggs and a cup of coffee or tea. Adjust the sweetness of the kaya according to your taste preferences by adding more or less sugar. You can also store any leftover kaya in an airtight container in the refrigerator for up to a week.

Arroz con Leche (Spain)

Ingredients:

- 1 cup short-grain rice (such as Arborio or Valencia rice)
- 4 cups whole milk
- 1/2 cup granulated sugar
- 1 cinnamon stick
- 1 strip of lemon zest
- Pinch of salt
- Ground cinnamon, for garnish

Instructions:

1. Rinse the rice under cold water until the water runs clear. Drain well.
2. In a large saucepan, combine the rinsed rice, whole milk, sugar, cinnamon stick, lemon zest, and a pinch of salt.
3. Place the saucepan over medium heat and bring the mixture to a gentle boil, stirring occasionally to prevent the rice from sticking to the bottom of the pan.
4. Once the mixture comes to a boil, reduce the heat to low and let it simmer gently, stirring occasionally, for about 30-40 minutes, or until the rice is tender and the mixture has thickened to a creamy consistency.
5. Remove the saucepan from the heat and discard the cinnamon stick and lemon zest.
6. Allow the Arroz con Leche to cool slightly before serving. You can serve it warm, at room temperature, or chilled, according to your preference.
7. To serve, spoon the Arroz con Leche into individual serving bowls and sprinkle with ground cinnamon for garnish.
8. Enjoy your homemade Arroz con Leche as a delicious and comforting dessert!

Note: You can customize the flavor of Arroz con Leche by adding ingredients such as vanilla extract, orange zest, or raisins during cooking. Adjust the sweetness according to your taste preference by adding more or less sugar. Leftovers can be stored in the refrigerator for up to 3-4 days.

Tortilla Española (Spain)Ingredients:

- 4-5 large eggs
- 3 medium potatoes, peeled and thinly sliced
- 1 onion, thinly sliced
- Salt, to taste
- Olive oil, for frying

Instructions:

1. Heat a generous amount of olive oil in a large non-stick skillet over medium heat.
2. Add the thinly sliced potatoes to the skillet in a single layer. Fry the potatoes, stirring occasionally, until they are tender but not browned, about 8-10 minutes.

3. Add the thinly sliced onions to the skillet with the potatoes. Continue to cook, stirring occasionally, until the onions are soft and translucent, about 5-6 minutes. Season with salt to taste.
4. While the potatoes and onions are cooking, crack the eggs into a large mixing bowl. Season with a pinch of salt and beat the eggs until well combined.
5. Once the potatoes and onions are cooked, use a slotted spoon to transfer them to the bowl with the beaten eggs. Stir gently to combine, making sure the potatoes and onions are evenly distributed in the egg mixture.
6. Drain most of the excess olive oil from the skillet, leaving just enough to coat the bottom.
7. Return the skillet to the heat and pour the egg, potato, and onion mixture into the skillet. Use a spatula to spread the mixture evenly in the skillet.
8. Cook the tortilla over medium-low heat, shaking the skillet occasionally to prevent sticking, until the bottom is golden brown and the edges start to set, about 6-8 minutes.
9. Once the bottom is golden brown, carefully flip the tortilla using a large plate or lid to cover the skillet. Slide the tortilla back into the skillet, uncooked side down.
10. Continue to cook the tortilla for another 4-6 minutes, or until the eggs are fully set and the tortilla is cooked through.
11. Once the tortilla is cooked to your liking, remove it from the skillet and transfer it to a cutting board. Allow it to cool for a few minutes before slicing into wedges.
12. Serve the Tortilla Española warm or at room temperature, garnished with fresh parsley if desired.
13. Enjoy your homemade Tortilla Española as a delicious and classic Spanish dish!

Note: Tortilla Española can be served as a tapa, appetizer, or main course, and it's delicious on its own or accompanied by a side salad or crusty bread. You can also customize the filling by adding ingredients such as bell peppers, chorizo, or cheese according to your taste preferences.

Pan con Tomate (Spain)

Ingredients:

- 1 large ripe tomato
- 1 clove garlic, peeled
- Extra virgin olive oil

- Pinch of salt
- Crusty bread, such as baguette or rustic country bread, sliced

Instructions:

1. Slice the ripe tomato in half horizontally. Use a grater or the large holes of a box grater to grate the cut side of the tomato into a bowl, discarding the skin.
2. Cut the clove of garlic in half horizontally. Rub the cut side of the garlic over the slices of bread, imparting a light garlic flavor. You can use more or less garlic according to your taste preference.
3. Drizzle a little extra virgin olive oil over each slice of bread, spreading it evenly with the back of a spoon or a pastry brush.
4. Spoon the grated tomato over the oiled and garlic-rubbed bread slices, spreading it evenly to cover the surface of each slice.
5. Sprinkle a pinch of salt over the tomato-topped bread slices, to taste.
6. Optionally, you can drizzle a little more extra virgin olive oil over the top of the tomato-topped bread slices for extra flavor.
7. Serve the Pan con Tomate immediately as a tapa or appetizer, alongside other Spanish dishes, or enjoy it as a snack.
8. Enjoy your homemade Pan con Tomate with its simple yet delicious combination of flavors!

Note: Pan con Tomate is best enjoyed fresh, shortly after assembling, while the bread is still crusty and the flavors are vibrant. You can customize the dish by adding toppings such as slices of cured ham (jamón), cheese, anchovies, or olives. Experiment with different types of bread and adjust the seasoning according to your taste preferences.

Welsh Rarebit (Wales)

Ingredients:

- 4 slices of thick-cut bread (such as sourdough or whole grain)
- 2 tablespoons unsalted butter
- 2 tablespoons all-purpose flour
- 1 teaspoon Dijon mustard

- 1/2 teaspoon Worcestershire sauce
- 1/2 teaspoon paprika
- 1/2 cup beer (such as ale or stout), at room temperature
- 2 cups grated sharp cheddar cheese
- Salt and black pepper, to taste
- Chopped fresh parsley or chives, for garnish (optional)

Instructions:

1. Preheat your oven to the broil setting.
2. Toast the slices of bread until they are lightly golden brown on both sides. You can toast them in a toaster or under the broiler in your oven. Once toasted, arrange the bread slices on a baking sheet and set aside.
3. In a saucepan, melt the butter over medium heat. Once melted, add the flour and whisk continuously to form a roux. Cook the roux for 1-2 minutes, stirring constantly, until it is smooth and bubbly.
4. Add the Dijon mustard, Worcestershire sauce, and paprika to the roux. Stir to combine.
5. Gradually pour in the beer, whisking constantly, until the mixture is smooth and well combined.
6. Reduce the heat to low and add the grated cheddar cheese to the saucepan, a handful at a time, stirring constantly until the cheese is melted and the sauce is smooth and creamy.
7. Season the cheese sauce with salt and black pepper to taste. Keep warm over low heat, stirring occasionally, while you prepare the bread.
8. Spoon the cheese sauce evenly over the toasted bread slices, making sure to cover each slice completely.
9. Place the baking sheet with the assembled Welsh Rarebit under the broiler and broil for 2-3 minutes, or until the cheese sauce is bubbly and lightly browned on top. Keep a close eye on it to prevent burning.
10. Remove the Welsh Rarebit from the oven and garnish with chopped fresh parsley or chives, if desired.
11. Serve the Welsh Rarebit hot, as a delicious and satisfying dish for breakfast, brunch, or a light lunch.
12. Enjoy your homemade Welsh Rarebit with its rich and cheesy flavor, served over crusty toasted bread!

Biscuits and Gravy (United States)

Ingredients:

For the biscuits:

- 2 cups all-purpose flour
- 1 tablespoon baking powder
- 1 teaspoon granulated sugar
- 1/2 teaspoon salt
- 1/2 cup unsalted butter, cold and cubed
- 3/4 cup buttermilk

For the sausage gravy:

- 1/2 pound breakfast sausage (pork or turkey)
- 2 tablespoons unsalted butter
- 1/4 cup all-purpose flour
- 2 cups whole milk
- Salt and black pepper, to taste

Instructions:

1. Preheat your oven to 425°F (220°C). Line a baking sheet with parchment paper or grease it lightly.
2. In a large mixing bowl, whisk together the all-purpose flour, baking powder, sugar, and salt until well combined.
3. Add the cold, cubed butter to the flour mixture. Use a pastry cutter or your fingers to work the butter into the flour until the mixture resembles coarse crumbs with pea-sized butter pieces.
4. Pour the buttermilk into the flour mixture and stir until just combined. Be careful not to overmix.
5. Turn the dough out onto a lightly floured surface. Gently pat or roll out the dough to about 1/2 inch thickness.
6. Use a biscuit cutter or a glass to cut out biscuits from the dough. Place the biscuits onto the prepared baking sheet, leaving a little space between each biscuit.
7. Gather any remaining dough scraps, gently pat them together, and cut out additional biscuits.

8. Bake the biscuits in the preheated oven for 12-15 minutes, or until they are golden brown on top and cooked through.
9. While the biscuits are baking, prepare the sausage gravy. In a large skillet, cook the breakfast sausage over medium heat, breaking it apart with a spatula, until it is browned and cooked through. Remove the cooked sausage from the skillet and set it aside.
10. In the same skillet, melt the butter over medium heat. Once melted, sprinkle the flour over the melted butter and whisk to combine. Cook the flour mixture, stirring constantly, for 1-2 minutes to cook off the raw flour taste.
11. Gradually pour the milk into the skillet, whisking constantly to prevent lumps from forming. Continue to cook the gravy, stirring frequently, until it thickens to your desired consistency, about 5-7 minutes.
12. Once the gravy has thickened, stir in the cooked breakfast sausage. Season the gravy with salt and black pepper to taste.
13. To serve, split the warm biscuits in half and place them on serving plates. Spoon the sausage gravy generously over the biscuits.
14. Enjoy your homemade Biscuits and Gravy as a delicious and comforting Southern-inspired breakfast or brunch dish!

Note: You can customize this recipe by using different types of sausage or adding herbs and spices to the biscuit dough or gravy according to your taste preferences.

Tex-Mex Migas (United States)Ingredients:

6 large eggs

4 corn tortillas, cut into strips

1 tablespoon vegetable oil

1/2 onion, diced

1/2 bell pepper (any color), diced

1 jalapeño pepper, seeded and diced (optional)

2 tomatoes, diced

1/2 cup shredded cheese (such as cheddar or Monterey Jack)

Salt and pepper, to taste

Chopped fresh cilantro, for garnish (optional)

Salsa, for serving (optional)

Avocado slices, for serving (optional)

Lime wedges, for serving (optional)

Instructions:

In a large mixing bowl, whisk the eggs together until well beaten. Season with salt and pepper to taste. Set aside.

Heat the vegetable oil in a large skillet over medium heat. Add the tortilla strips and cook, stirring occasionally, until they are golden brown and crispy, about 5-7 minutes. Remove the tortilla strips from the skillet and set them aside on a plate lined with paper towels to drain excess oil.

In the same skillet, add the diced onion, bell pepper, and jalapeño pepper (if using). Cook, stirring occasionally, until the vegetables are softened, about 3-4 minutes.

Add the diced tomatoes to the skillet and cook for another 2-3 minutes, until they are slightly softened.

Pour the beaten eggs into the skillet with the cooked vegetables. Stir gently to combine, then let the eggs cook undisturbed for a minute or two until they start to set around the edges.

Using a spatula, gently scramble the eggs, stirring occasionally, until they are cooked to your desired consistency.

Once the eggs are cooked, add the crispy tortilla strips to the skillet. Sprinkle the shredded cheese over the top of the eggs and tortillas. Stir gently to combine and allow the cheese to melt.

Remove the skillet from the heat. Taste and adjust seasoning with salt and pepper if needed.

Serve the Tex-Mex Migas hot, garnished with chopped fresh cilantro if desired. Serve with salsa, avocado slices, and lime wedges on the side, if desired.

Enjoy your homemade Tex-Mex Migas as a delicious and satisfying breakfast or brunch dish with a southwestern flair!

Note: Feel free to customize this recipe by adding other ingredients such as cooked chorizo, black beans, or green onions. Adjust the level of spiciness by adding more or fewer jalapeño peppers, or by including hot sauce or chili powder to the eggs.

Cuban Sandwich (Cuba)

Ingredients:

- 1 loaf Cuban bread or French bread, cut into sandwich-sized portions and sliced lengthwise
- 1/2 pound roast pork, thinly sliced
- 1/4 pound ham, thinly sliced
- 4 slices Swiss cheese
- Dill pickles, thinly sliced lengthwise
- Yellow mustard, to taste
- Butter or margarine, softened

Instructions:

1. Preheat a sandwich press, panini press, or a large skillet over medium heat.
2. Spread a thin layer of mustard on one side of each bread slice.
3. Layer the bottom half of each bread portion with slices of roast pork, followed by slices of ham, Swiss cheese, and dill pickles.
4. Place the top half of the bread on top of the fillings to form sandwiches.
5. Spread a thin layer of butter or margarine on the outside of each sandwich.
6. Place the sandwiches on the preheated sandwich press, panini press, or skillet. If using a skillet, you can press the sandwiches down with a spatula or another heavy pan to flatten them slightly.
7. Cook the sandwiches for 3-5 minutes on each side, or until the bread is crispy and golden brown and the cheese is melted.

8. Once the sandwiches are cooked to your liking, remove them from the heat and let them cool slightly before serving.
9. Cut the sandwiches in half diagonally and serve them hot.
10. Enjoy your homemade Cuban Sandwiches as a delicious and satisfying meal!

Note: Traditional Cuban Sandwiches use Cuban bread, which is a type of long, fluffy bread with a crispy crust. If you can't find Cuban bread, you can use French bread or another type of crusty bread as a substitute. You can also customize the fillings by adding ingredients such as sliced salami, roasted red peppers, or onions according to your taste preferences.

Colombian Arepas (Colombia)

Ingredients:

- 2 cups pre-cooked white cornmeal (masarepa)
- 2 cups warm water
- 1 teaspoon salt
- 1 tablespoon vegetable oil (optional)
- Additional vegetable oil, for cooking

Instructions:

1. In a large mixing bowl, combine the pre-cooked white cornmeal (masarepa) and salt.
2. Gradually add the warm water to the cornmeal mixture, stirring continuously, until a soft dough forms. The dough should be smooth and pliable, similar to playdough.
3. Once the dough comes together, knead it gently for a few minutes until it is well combined. If the dough feels too dry, you can add a little more warm water, a tablespoon at a time, until it reaches the right consistency. If the dough feels too wet, you can add a little more cornmeal.
4. Divide the dough into 8-10 equal portions and roll each portion into a ball.

5. Flatten each ball of dough into a disk, about 1/4 to 1/2 inch thick, using your hands. You can also use a tortilla press or the bottom of a heavy flat-bottomed pan to flatten the dough.
6. Optional step: Brush each flattened arepa with a little vegetable oil on both sides. This will help them develop a crispy exterior when cooked.
7. Heat a non-stick skillet or griddle over medium heat. Once hot, add a little vegetable oil to the skillet to prevent sticking.
8. Place the flattened arepas in the skillet and cook for 4-5 minutes on each side, or until they are golden brown and crispy on the outside and cooked through in the middle. You may need to cook them in batches, depending on the size of your skillet.
9. Once cooked, transfer the arepas to a plate lined with paper towels to drain any excess oil.
10. Serve the Colombian Arepas warm, either on their own or stuffed with your favorite fillings. Common fillings include cheese, ham, avocado, eggs, beans, or shredded beef.
11. Enjoy your homemade Colombian Arepas as a delicious and versatile dish that can be enjoyed for breakfast, lunch, or dinner!

Note: Colombian Arepas can be stored in an airtight container in the refrigerator for up to 2-3 days. To reheat, simply warm them in a skillet over medium heat or in the microwave until heated through.

Venezuelan Arepas (Venezuela)

Ingredients:

- 2 cups pre-cooked white cornmeal (masarepa)
- 2 1/2 cups warm water
- 1 teaspoon salt
- 1 tablespoon vegetable oil
- Additional vegetable oil, for cooking

Instructions:

1. In a large mixing bowl, combine the pre-cooked white cornmeal (masarepa) and salt.

2. Gradually add the warm water to the cornmeal mixture, stirring continuously, until a soft dough forms. The dough should be smooth and pliable, similar to playdough.
3. Once the dough comes together, knead it gently for a few minutes until it is well combined. If the dough feels too dry, you can add a little more warm water, a tablespoon at a time, until it reaches the right consistency. If the dough feels too wet, you can add a little more cornmeal.
4. Divide the dough into 8-10 equal portions and roll each portion into a ball.
5. Flatten each ball of dough into a disk, about 1/2 inch thick, using your hands. You can also use a tortilla press or the bottom of a heavy flat-bottomed pan to flatten the dough.
6. Heat a non-stick skillet or griddle over medium heat. Once hot, add a little vegetable oil to the skillet to prevent sticking.
7. Place the flattened arepas in the skillet and cook for 4-5 minutes on each side, or until they are golden brown and crispy on the outside and cooked through in the middle. You may need to cook them in batches, depending on the size of your skillet.
8. Once cooked, transfer the arepas to a plate lined with paper towels to drain any excess oil.
9. Once the arepas are cool enough to handle, slice them open horizontally using a serrated knife, being careful not to cut all the way through.
10. Fill each arepa with your desired fillings, such as cheese, meats, avocado, beans, or eggs.
11. Serve the Venezuelan Arepas warm and enjoy their delicious and versatile flavors!

Note: Venezuelan Arepas can be stored in an airtight container in the refrigerator for up to 2-3 days. To reheat, simply warm them in a skillet over medium heat or in the microwave until heated through. Experiment with different fillings to create your own unique arepa creations!